Sir John Summerson is
among the greatest of English architectural historians.
Curator of Sir John Soane's Museum from 1945 until his
retirement in 1984, he had been Slade Professor of Fine Art
at both Oxford and Cambridge and had lectured on the
history of architecture at Birkbeck College, London. He died
in 1992. Of his many books, the best known are probably
Georgian London and *Architecture in Britain 1530-1830*,
both standard works.

WORLD OF ART

This famous series
provides the widest available
range of illustrated books on art in all its aspects.
If you would like to receive a complete list
of titles in print please write to:
THAMES AND HUDSON
30 Bloomsbury Street, London WC1B 3QP
In the United States please write to:
THAMES AND HUDSON INC.
500 Fifth Avenue, New York, New York 10110

Printed in Spain

The Architecture of
the Eighteenth Century

JOHN SUMMERSON

with 174 illustrations

THAMES AND HUDSON

© 1969 and 1986 Thames and Hudson Ltd, London
Parts of this book first appeared as
'The Architectural Setting: Royalty, religion
and the urban background'
in Alfred Cobban (ed.), *The Eighteenth Century:
Europe in the Age of Enlightenment*
(London, and New York, 1969)

First published in the World of Art series in 1986
Reprinted 1996

ISBN 0-500-20202-8

Printed and bound in Spain by Artes Graficas Toledo S.A.
D.L.T.O.: 348-1996

Contents

CHAPTER ONE

The Ascendancy and Fall of the Baroque

Approaching 18th-century architecture as a continuous performance, abruptly curtained at 1700 and 1800, one seeks, in self-defence, some shaping generalizations. Here are two. (i) The first half of the century was pervaded by the spirit and forms of the Baroque, while the second half was the age of Neo-classicism. (ii) The characteristic building types of the first half of the century were churches and palaces, while those of the second half were public and institutional buildings. The first generalization is about style, the second about building types. They are complementary. Their usefulness is in their vagueness, and however much their pretensions dissolve on closer examination, they are still not meaningless.

Style is what immediately takes the eye, excites curiosity and creates a receptive mood. So let us take our stylistic generalization first. What are we really talking about when we say 'Baroque' and 'Neo-classical'? Let us not pretend that either of these modern expressions can have a precise meaning. They evoke a certain emotional predisposition to what is being talked of and that is useful. Beyond that, the meaning must emerge in the course of exposition and in the comparison of the unfamiliar with the familiar. In the case of the Baroque, the familiar, for most people, belongs to the century preceding that with which we are concerned. What happened in Rome between Maderno's completion of the west front of St Peter's in 1613 and the death of Bernini in 1680 was of high importance to European architecture for at least two generations, though important in curiously different ways – sometimes in inspired acceptance, elsewhere in contemptuous rejection. These conspicuous happenings are connected with the careers of three men – Pietro da Cortona,

1 S. Andrea al Quirinale, 1658–70, by Gian Lorenzo Bernini. The architecture of the early 18th century was inspired by the great Baroque creations of the late 17th. S. Andrea is one of these. The oval plan, giant portal and swirling lines echo in the later Baroque of Central Europe.

2 The Palazzo Odescalchi, Rome, begun 1664. Bernini was the presiding genius of the Baroque in Italy and his palace façades, with their formidable ranks of pilasters and deeply shadowing cornices, were among his legacies to the courts of 18th-century Europe.

3 S. Carlo alle Quattro Fontane; the façade of 1665–67, by Francesco Borromini. Borromini's studied distortions of the classical elements and the play of convex against concave were to reappear transmuted in the Rococo architecture of the north.

4 Right: The dome of S. Lorenzo, Turin, 1668–87, by Guarino Guarini. Planned on an eight-pointed star, the free-standing arches bring ideas from Islamic sources into the Baroque quest for the poetry of light.

Francesco Borromini and Gian Lorenzo Bernini himself. They, with Maderno, are the masters to whom posterity has learnt most especially to apply the word Baroque. Unlike as can be in their personal styles, they share a grandiloquence of statement, a mobility and sweep of invention which made them irresistible in their time and a challenge to every northerner who crossed the Alps thereafter. They summed up the whole past. They were the masters, not the slaves, of antiquity; they were the legatees of Michelangelo; they were the latest actors on the scene set by Bramante.

The Legacy of Roman Baroque

When we cross the datum of 1700 the Roman Baroque scene must constantly be in our minds. Constantly, we shall be reminded in south German churches of the plan-shapes devised by Borromini; often, in palaces, of the Roman façades of Bernini and the designs he made for the Louvre. An important point is that the Baroque masters were not looked back upon as academic models, to be imitated. They were liberators, and the barriers they had broken were thrust down even further by the adventurous masters of central Europe – by Fischer von Erlach, the Dientzenhofers, Hildebrandt, Neumann, the Asams and Pöppelmann. In particular the originalities of Borromini, who tore apart the conventions of Bramantesque classicism and reassembled the

9

fragments in results of shocking vitality, were the signals for these spatial adventures.

Now, the acceptance of Roman Baroque is scarcely less important in the history of 18th-century architecture than its total rejection. A significant instance is that of Colen Campbell, the Scotsman, who, writing in London in 1715, declared that the Italians had lost all taste for architecture in the pursuit of capricious novelties. Borromini was basest of all. He had 'endeavoured to debauch Mankind with his odd and chimerical Beauties, where the Parts are without Proportion, Solids without their true Bearing, Heaps of Materials without Strength, excessive Ornaments without Grace, and the Whole without Symmetry'.

The Scotsman's rude intrusion brings us sharply to our next question – the meaning of Neo-classicism. In so forcibly condemning the Roman Baroque as wrong, what did Campbell recommend as right? The answer is simple. The foundations of architecture, he said, were in antiquity and the classic expositor of antiquity was Vitruvius; Vitruvius had found a modern interpreter of genius in Palladio; in England one architect and one only had understood this – Inigo Jones. So there was a triple loyalty – Vitruvius, Palladio, Jones – embodying (at least for the English) all architectural truth. Campbell supported his philosophy with the works (including his own) which he selected for his publication, *Vitruvius Britannicus*. He did not argue its merits at any length – merely stated, even rather naïvely, a view which he was confident would, in the England of 1715, be accepted. It was.

It would be wrong, of course, to assume either that Campbell's views are a precise reflection of the Neo-classical idea or that such views originated in Britain. What *is* Neo-classical in Campbell is his conviction that it was important, as he says. 'to judge truly of the Merit of Things by the Strength of Reason'. For Campbell, antiquity was rational and its revival was an abuse if its rationality was not respected. This view was not new. A literal acceptance of the antique as embodying all fundamental wisdom about building had been received in France and debated in French intellectual circles for a long time – at least sincc the foundation of Louis XIV's Académie Royale d'Architecture in 1672. Here the controversies between the 'Ancients' and the 'Moderns' had involved the head of the Académie, François

Blondel, and the architect mainly credited with the east front of the Louvre, Claude Perrault. Perrault's annotated edition of Vitruvius on the one hand and Blondel's *Cours d'Architecture* on the other were texts which led to continuous debate and to the rapid propagation of the idea that there were vital distinctions to be made in the cultivation of classical architecture. The distinctions were, approximately, between a rational and a literal use of the antique – 'rational' here implying a conception of the antique as having evolved out of building needs and being therefore capable of continued modification, and 'literal' implying an acceptance of antique forms as unalterable absolutes. Naturally, neither school of thought ever secured a real victory over the other; the important thing is that these arguments were sustained. The roots of Neo-classicism are intellectual, they grew in the asking of questions. As we enter the 18th century we shall find the questions being answered, and answered mainly where they were first asked – in France.

The part played by France in 18th-century architecture is not as obvious as is sometimes thought. Paris certainly enjoyed enormous authority throughout the century, but this was to a great extent carried on the momentum of Colbert's unparalleled triumphs under Louis XIV. The works of François Mansart and Le Vau – the Louvre and Versailles, Marly, the Collège Mazarin, the Invalides, the Place des Victoires, the Place Vendôme – had given Paris absolute architectural precedence in Europe. But all these belong to the 17th century, running a few years into the 18th. The dominating architectural personality of the last phase – Jules Hardouin-Mansart – died in 1708. Then followed a period of thirty or forty years during which French architecture, in its general deportment, scarcely moved. The Académie and the Royal Works were in the hands of men who had been Mansart's pupils or worked under him. Robert de Cotte was his immediate successor as *premier architecte*, Germain Boffrand the other most influential personality. These men embodied and pre-served a tradition – the tradition which is perhaps best called French Classicism and which has its roots in de Brosse, the elder Mansart and Le Vau. They could, on occasion, be original and powerfully eloquent.

They did sometimes very nearly, but never quite, become Baroque.

Three buildings of 17th-century France that represent a reasoned classicism in contrast to the daring innovations of Italian Baroque.

5 Perrault's east front of the Louvre, begun 1667.

6 Church of the Invalides by Jules Hardouin-Mansart, 1680–91.

7 Top right: The palace of Versailles, with the huge wings added by Hardouin-Mansart towards the end of the century.

Their loyalty was to their antecedents and the test of loyalty was *le bon goût*. *Le bon goût* was an affair of combining common sense with acute sensibility, opposing mere fashion and proceeding (as Boffrand rather platitudinously put it) as far as possible from the good towards the excellent.

In this attitude was preserved the authority of the *grand siècle* with all its accomplishment but little of its ambition or invention, for which there were indeed, few opportunities. It was important, however, that the authority was there; French classicism remained a living force which was respected and frequently consulted throughout Europe. Only in England, wholly obsessed with the Vitruvius–Palladio–Jones equation was its authority ignored.

Rococo and rationalism

Having said that French architecture of the decades following the death of Louis XIV moved very little, it must now be observed that in one particular direction it moved very briskly. This was in the invention of the Rococo. The style started quite distinctly as a grotesquely mannered version of Louis XIV interior decoration. This was disembodied and endowed with the aerial quality of antique arabesques. The heavy scrolls of the old style became snaky S-curves; the cumbrous panels dissolved into tenuous *boiseries*. Then came a phase of greater intensity. A brilliant young apprentice of Hardouin-

13

Mansart called Gilles Marie Oppenordt was sent to the French Academy in Rome in 1692. There, instead of concentrating on the antique, he cultivated the marginal eccentricities of Borromini and returned to Paris with a singular knack of making the subsidiaries in a decorative scheme so energetic that the framework became redundant. Once this possibility had been disclosed there was no end to its development – no end, at least, until in the middle of the century, in the rising tide of Neo-classicism, it was laughed out of existence. For a time it was accepted in France even by men like de Cotte and Boffrand (for interiors and garden buildings only); the great exponents after Oppenordt were Meissonnier and Cuvilliès. Cuvilliès took the style to Munich, where it flourished into a school, distinctly different from what had been accepted in Paris and with a spectacular radiance. Every court in Europe had its Rococo phase. Even England was not totally immune; and there is some pretty Rococo in Ireland.

But apart from the grand manner of French Classicism and apart from the invention of Rococo there was something else going on in France in the early years of the century, barely noticed at the time but of far greater importance for the future. This was a new philosophical radicalism which emerged from the theoretical debating of what constituted a rational architecture. The first clear, totally radical, voice was that of the Abbé de Cordemoy who, in 1706, published his *Nouveau Traité de toute l'Architecture*. In this, he proposed a system of a revolutionary kind. The whole Renaissance tradition of architectural expression by the modelling of façades into *representations* of architecture (e.g. pilasters, half-columns, false pediments) was to be dethroned. More than that, arches were to be abandoned. Architecture was to return to what Cordemoy conceived to be the Greek mode – and the Greek limitations. It was to be column-and-lintel architecture, with rigorous articulation of all elements and little or no ornament.

A philosophy of this sort issuing in what was still the age of Jules-Hardouin Mansart could not be expected to have a very immediate impact on practical architecture. Cordemoy, however, had issued a challenge which was full of meaning. In a way it was like the challenge of the Rococo – but an opposite sort of challenge. The Rococo offered an immediate visual escape from tradition into a free world of linear romance; and Rococo was allowed to roam delightfully and safely in the salons and galleries. Cordemoy's theory offered no way of escape short of an undermining of the whole tradition of academic rules and *le bon goût*.

The eventual outcome of Cordemoy's thesis was the explosion of opinion in the middle of the century set off by another French cleric, the Abbé Laugier, whose *Essai sur l'Architecture* of 1752, borrowing extensively from Cordemoy, became immediately popular, was translated into English and German, and was a textbook for those various lines of development which we now bracket together under the heading of Neo-classicism. Neo-classicism involves, as we shall see, far more than textbook theories. It involves archaeological investigation on the one hand and a release of imaginative invention on the other; it involves the puritanism of the English Palladians and the vertiginous romancing of Piranesi. But at the centre of it all is the Cordemoy-Laugier thesis of architecture as a totally rational system – as arguably functional as the wooden cabin which primitive man may be conceived to have built to keep himself dry. The germ of thought released by Cordemoy into the Renaissance-Baroque world of 1706 multiplied itself into a force which survived the extinction of that world and, in the long run, re-orientated architecture in a way which made the uneasy revolutions of the 19th century inevitable and the conclusions of the 20th possible.

8 The Abbé Laugier's concept of the origins of architecture as shown in the frontispiece of his *Essai sur l'Architecture*, 1755: the 'primitive cabin' formed by assembling tree trunks and branches. The hypothesis was as old as Vitruvius, but Laugier used it to project his theory that columns should declare their function and that pilasters and all 'architecture in relief' was irrational nonsense.

CHAPTER TWO

The Architecture of Absolutism

Putting all this into the fewest possible words, we have seen that the 17th century bequeathed the Baroque to the 18th, but that the Baroque was then assaulted from the outside by radical theories of a rational kind and eroded from the inside by mutations of its own nature. Let us now turn to some of the buildings in which these processes are seen to be at work. First, palaces.

Three royal palaces: Vienna, Stockholm and Berlin

In 1700, three great royal palaces were being built – in Vienna, Stockholm and Berlin. If we glance at the incentives behind these, and consider the architectural results, we shall understand something of the nature of palace-building in the 18th century. Take Vienna first. Under the Emperor Leopold I the city finally disposed of the Ottoman menace and after the Relief of Vienna in 1683 there was a surge of optimism and national consciousness at once reflected in building activity. The two grand criteria for the builders were Paris and Rome and by 1691 a Viennese writer was boasting that the city surpassed the first and at least equalled the second. In 1695 the imperial palace of Schönbrunn was begun. It was outside the city – a Viennese Versailles – and the clear intention was to invest the imperial dignity with a symbol no less striking than Versailles. The architect was J. B. Fischer von Erlach, the son of a mason–sculptor and himself first a sculptor, who had spent twelve years in Italy. A clue to his attitude and to the atmosphere in which he worked is given by the remarkable book which he published towards the end of his life, the *Entwurf einer historischen Architektur* (1721). It is a pictorial history of the world's architecture containing besides reconstructions of the seven wonders

9 Staircase of the Palace of Caserta, near Naples, 1751–74, by Luigi Vanvitelli (for plan see pl. 32). Staircases came into their own with the Baroque, consuming extravagant quantities of space for the sake of sheer architectural display.

17

10, 11 Schönbrunn, the Viennese Versailles, was begun in 1695, raising the Emperor Leopold to equality with Louis XIV. His architect was J. B. Fischer von Erlach, and it was to Bernini that he turned for inspiration. The garden front, seen here in a painting by Bellotto of 1759, was altered in 1744–49, but the long parade of pilasters is Fischer's. In the background is the city of Vienna, with Fischer's Karlskirche (pl. 34, 35) on the right. In 1721 Fischer had published a series of engravings to illustrate the history of world architecture, *Entwurf einer historischen Architektur*, though his purpose was 'to inspire the artist rather than inform the scholar'. This view of Nero's Golden House in Rome (right) is close to Schönbrunn, and would have been closer had his original plans been realized.

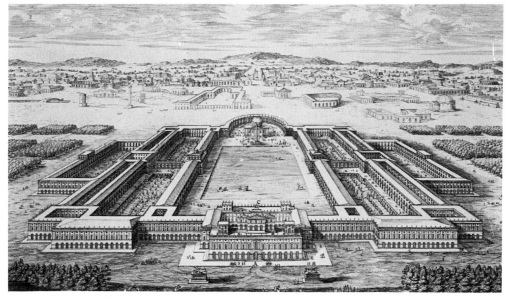

12, 13 The Royal Palace of Berlin, begun for Frederick I, King of Prussia in 1698, by Andreas Schlüter, stood at the heart of the new king's new capital. One side (above), its monotonous lines of windows broken only by bays with columns, faced a ceremonial square. The entrance (left), later crowned by a dome, fronted the river.

of the world, all sorts of unexpected things, such as Stonehenge, Santa Sophia at Constantinople and the city of Peking. To these are added splendid engravings of Fischer's own works. It is obviously the composition of a man who saw himself at the very apex of all architectural performance up to his time.

Schönbrunn echoes Versailles in its plan, its great gallery and likewise in the lengthy (but not nearly so nauseatingly so) parade of pilasters on the garden front. It also seems to echo Fischer's idea, as he gives it to us in his book, of what the Golden House of Nero looked like in antiquity. In other words, one might say that Schönbrunn is politically connected with Versailles and romantically with imperial Rome.

Rome and Paris, Paris and Rome – these were the foci of the architects' imaginations – though Rome meant Bernini more often than it meant the Caesars. This we see at Stockholm. Charles XI of

14 The Royal Palace of Stockholm, begun by Charles XII of Sweden in 1697, with Nicodemus Tessin as his architect. Tessin had worked in Rome under Bernini, and Roman Baroque was his model here, combined with recollections of the Louvre.

Sweden had, in 1693, been explicitly recognized as holding supreme power and with a long series of military successes behind him an analogy with Louis XIV was not fatuous. Moreover, Charles had reduced the power of the Swedish aristocracy (as Louis had the French); his absolutism was of a kind which enforced the expediency of a powerfully representational setting. He was not a man of much culture but he had a remarkable architect – Nicodemus Tessin II. Son of an earlier court architect, Tessin had studied in Rome under Bernini and had visited Paris in 1687. He was soon set to reorganize the old Royal Castle at Stockholm but in 1697 this was burnt down. In the same year Charles XI died and in the peaceful first three years of Charles XII a new royal palace began to rise. Being a town palace the model was the Louvre: the great court at Stockholm is about two thirds the size of that of the Louvre. The exterior architecture however is not French, but Roman Baroque, of a kind more loyal to its origins than any palace of central Europe. Bernini's Odescalchi and Labacco's Sciarra Palace are gravely quoted on its main façades. The interiors were delayed by Charles XII's wars but they are mostly French. Tessin brought in French decorators and craftsmen and after his death in 1728 his son continued the French ways. But it is as a Roman Baroque monument, a little out of time and far out of place, that the Royal Palace dominates, as massive and flat as the Quirinal Palace, the city of Stockholm.

Berlin may well owe something to the Stockholm palace. Here, the incentive was the ambition of the Elector of Brandenburg, Frederick III, to acquire the style of King. He did so, in 1701, as Frederick I, King of Prussia. The building of a Louvre was a desirable preliminary. For this he employed Andreas Schlüter, a sculptor-architect of genius whose origins and early life in Warsaw are obscure. Schlüter planned a huge rectangle consisting of two courts, longer than the Louvre though not as wide (but exactly the width of Stockholm). He only succeeded in building one court before his dismissal as a result of the collapse of a too ambitious tower. The Berlin palace is no more; it was deliberately destroyed for political reasons (the reasons, in another context, for which it was built) in 1945.

With these three palaces – Vienna, Stockholm, Berlin – it is instructive to compare a palace that was never built. In 1698 the old Palace of Whitehall in London was (like the old Castle in Stockholm in the previous year) destroyed by fire. Immediately, the King's surveyor, Sir Christopher Wren, prepared plans for a new palace covering the whole site and incorporating the Banqueting House of Inigo Jones, which had survived. That the palace was never built is not surprising: absolutism in England was extinct. But the plans remain as a project of extraordinary originality – less accomplished, to be sure, than Fischer or Tessin or Schlüter, but wonderfully expressive in their dramatic articulation. As at Stockholm, and to some extent at Berlin, the influence of Gian Lorenzo Bernini shines through.

The Courts of Germany

These three – or, counting Whitehall, four – royal palaces conceived at the turn of the century introduce an age of palace-building lasting for fifty years. Always it is Paris and Rome which supply the basic concepts (and sometimes, indeed, the architects) but in the German-speaking lands there emerged a few men of outstanding genius who conducted the Baroque idea into new and original paths. Three of these men were born within a few years of each other. Mathaeus Daniel Pöppelmann, a Westphalian who came to Dresden, was born in 1662. Johann Lukas von Hildebrandt of Vienna was born in 1663 and so was Johann Dientzenhofer, one of a family of architects in Prague who came to Bavaria and Franconia. If we seek names to set beside these outside central Europe we find in Italy nobody and in France only Germain Boffrand, born in 1667, and he was almost wholly integrated in the Mansart tradition; but if we cast our net as wide as England there are Sir John Vanbrugh, born in 1664, and his collaborator, Nicholas Hawksmoor, born in 1661, who in spirit and even sometimes in form are singularly close to their German and Austrian contemporaries.

Of these names, Hildebrandt's becomes first the important one. He was an architect of a new type. The son of a German captain in the Genoese army he had no craft background but became a pupil of Carlo Fontana in Rome and studied military engineering. His great work is the Upper Belvedere built for Prince Eugene in 1721–22. Hildebrandt followed Fischer in many things but not in his romantic attachment to history. He was very much a contemporary designer, rarely using the conventional orders and achieving his effects by brilliant play with Baroque and Mannerist ornaments he had seen in Genoa and Turin. Then, Hildebrandt's Baroque dissolves swiftly into Rococo. His ornaments become the substance, as they do in the French Rococo of Oppenordt. The staircase at the Belvedere has no orders. The piers of the lower hall are crouching giants; the vault over the stair itself rises from 'terms' with human torsos; and the lines of the structure swim into a free play of plaster relief ornament. The exterior is necessarily more rigid but the glamorous modelling of every part exorcizes the rigidity of convention. Hildebrandt invented the Austrian Baroque-Rococo equation and it is seen in the Belvedere in full maturity.

Hildebrandt's work leads us easily to that of Pöppelmann and to his fantastic performance in the Zwinger at Dresden. Plans for a palace for Augustus the Strong, challenging Stockholm and Berlin, were made soon after he came to the electoral throne of Saxony in 1694. But wars delayed the project till 1709. By then Pöppelmann had taken over. He was sent on a study trip to Vienna and Rome in 1710 and the building of the Zwinger proceeded; the Kronentor was built in 1713 and the Wall-pavilion begun in 1716. The Zwinger is only part of a palace and a subsidiary part at that, its sole purpose being as a theatre for tournaments with a 'grand-stand' (the Wall-pavilion) and a cere-monial gateway (the Kronentor). But there is probably no building in

15, 16 The Upper Belvedere in Vienna was built for Prince Eugene, 1721–22, by Fischer von Erlach's successor, Lukas von Hildebrandt. With its broken silhouette, playful centrepiece and domed pavilions, it already looks forward to the Rococo. In the entrance hall the grotesque 'atlantides' supporting the vault introduce an element of fantasy that recurs throughout German Baroque.

17 The Zwinger, in Dresden, in an 18th-century painting by Bellotto. The Zwinger was an open space for tournaments and court celebrations beside the palace. Its architect was Mathaeus Daniel Pöppelmann, but the result owes at least as much to the sculpture of Balthasar Permoser.

Europe since the Middle Ages where architecture and sculpture are combined with such immediacy. The architectural lines are remarkably rigid and in the proportions of the orders there is no serious distortion; but the architecture is deftly disintegrated to meet the flow of sculpture. The sculpture is the work of Balthasar Permoser but from the point of view of total effect it is difficult to judge where the architect stops and the sculptor begins. Virtually destroyed by bombs in 1944, the Zwinger has been successfully rebuilt.

The incentives to create a building of this kind are, in the case of the Zwinger, fairly obvious if we consider the almost ludicrous dynastic dreams of Augustus the Strong who, not content with Saxony, got himself elected King of Poland, losing and regaining that throne before his death in 1733. The patronage of personalities of this kind demanded nothing more profound than instant spectacle and spectacle of the utmost brilliance was what they got. Building was part of the power-game, which for an absolute ruler of psychotic energy like Augustus was the only game worth playing.

26

The mania for extravagant building we meet at every point in the age of palace-building. We meet it, for instance, at Pommersfelden, near Bamberg, where the Elector-Archbishop of Mainz – not, after all, a very consequential prince – confessed to an infatuation with architecture: 'building is a craze which costs much, but every fool likes his own hat'. Pommersfelden was designed by Johann Dientzenhofer, though not without the help of Hildebrandt, who was responsible for the staircase. It was built in 1711–18.

It is in a house like this – not on the greatest royal scale – that one is drawn to consider the relationships of German Baroque with the two greatest houses of Sir John Vanbrugh – Castle Howard (begun 1699) and Blenheim Palace (begun 1705). There can be no question of derivation and yet the same spatial enterprise is there. Compare Dientzenhofer's immensely tall pairs of Corinthian columns, pushing up into the pediment and breaking it, with Vanbrugh's pairs of Corinthian piers at Blenheim pushing through the pediment to break even more violently the pediment of the hall. Compare, again, the way the Pommersfelden staircase is conceived as an independent cage, as is the hall at Castle Howard, though the one contains the stair while the other penetrates staircases on each side. One must suppose that architects of similar age (as Vanbrugh and Dientzenhofer and, indeed, Hildebrandt were) intuitively seek, in a given situation, similar emergences – even if they view that situation from opposite ends of Europe.

The whole question of Baroque forms as understood by German architects comes most acutely to the fore when we reach the works of an architect more than twenty years younger than those we have been considering – Balthasar Neumann, who was born in 1687. Like Hildebrandt (and, for that matter, Vanbrugh) Neumann had some military experience before being taken into the service of the newly elected Prince-Bishop of Würzburg, who happened to be a Schönborn, one of the same family of prodigious builders to which the builder of Pommersfelden belonged. The Bishop had the same gargantuan passion for building and started the colossal Residenz at Würzburg in 1719. Neumann was his executant but the design passed through many hands, notably those of the great Boffrand in Paris and Hildebrandt in Vienna. Versailles, Schönbrunn and the Upper

18, 19 Pommersfelden was built for an Archbishop-Elector of Mainz, 1711–18, by Johann Dientzenhofer, with a staircase (right) by Hildebrandt. The staircase is an arcaded 'cage' in the centre of the house.

20, 21 Two English palaces by Sir John Vanbrugh – Blenheim and Castle Howard. Like Pommersfelden, Blenheim (below left) uses a giant Corinthian order, but based on the ground and supporting an orthodox pediment. The stairhall at Castle Howard (below right) is, like that at Pommersfelden, a stone 'cage', but the stairs rise outside, not inside the 'cage'.

22, 23 The Residenz at Würzburg, perhaps the most magnificent of all the German palaces. Begun in 1719 by Balthasar Neumann, it brought together some of the finest talents in Europe. The staircase ceiling (right) was painted by Gianbattista Tiepolo in 1737. He also decorated the Kaisersaal.

Belvedere are all reflected in this, the most majestic and accomplished of all German palaces. Neumann's own genius is especially conspicuous in the staircase which ascends in a single flight from a low, vaulted hall, dimly lit, then switches back in two narrower flights emerging in a hall over which floats one vast and fabulously brilliant painting by Tiepolo.

After Neumann, whose churches belong to a later section, the achievements of German Baroque – the counterparts in architecture of Bach and Handel in music – could hardly ascend further. Nevertheless, there is that ever-busy side-issue of the Baroque – the Rococo. This flourished supremely in Bavaria, thanks to the Elector Max Emanuel's discovery of genius in a French dwarf, François de Cuvilliès, who was born in 1695. He had him trained in Paris, then appointed him joint architect to his Court in Munich. The first purely Rococo pieces in Germany, distinct from the Baroque-Rococo of Hildebrandt, were the Reichen Zimmer in the Munich Residenz (1730–37). Then followed the summer pavilion known as the Amalienburg in the park at Nymphenburg. Here Cuvilliés brought

24, 25 Rococo is a style of architectural ornament of such incremental vigour that it tends to identify with the building it adorns. It is distinguished by undulating movement, counter-balancing curves, the use of 'rocaille' ornament evocative of coral and sea-shells – the whole as light in colour as in substance. These two examples are by François Cuvilliés: the Amalienburg Pavilion and the Reichenzimmer in the Residenz in Munich.

Rococo decoration to a kind of naturalism which it never achieved in France; it was almost as if Rococo themes, artificially planted, had begun to grow of themselves. Here and in the Munich Residenz-theater (see p. 103) are the models of the finest German Rococo. Through his colleagues and imitators and through Cuvilliés' own engravings the style spread throughout Germany and beyond.

Varieties of absolutism

In 1740, a monarch of equal celebrity as a political force, a military genius and a patron of the arts, succeeded to a German throne.

Frederick II of Prussia had already revolted against the philistinism of his father's Court and taken as his architect the patrician Georg Wenzeslaus von Knobelsdorff. The King and his architect worked closely together, Frederick actually making sketch plans which Knobelsdorff interpreted in the light of his own talents, which were considerable. He had been to Rome and, moreover, had mastered decorative art to the extent of being the author of the effective Rococo in the wing he added to Charlottenburg, one of his first works for the King. His next work, in 1741, was the Berlin Opera-House, a building which abruptly introduced into the Baroque scene an unexpected influence – English Palladianism. Frederick looked to England again when, years later, after Knobelsdorff's death, he built the Neues Palais at Potsdam – a rather sad derivative of Castle Howard. Meanwhile, the Stadtschloss at Potsdam showed an inclination towards Perrault's Louvre, while Sans Souci, the King's very personal summer residence at Potsdam, built in 1745–47, looked several ways at once. The entrance court with its Corinthian colonnades shows Knobelsdorff's tendency to a purer classicism. The garden front with its domed projecting centre is very evidently of Parisian derivation though the 'terms' which support its entablature might, in their extreme Rococo

26 Frederick the Great's palace of Sans Souci, at Potsdam, combines suggestions from a wide variety of sources, French and German (the caryatids supporting the entablature, for instance, recall the Zwinger). The architect was Georg von Knobelsdorff, the date 1740.

animation, have come from the Zwinger at Dresden. The interiors of
Sans Souci are similarly mixed. There is Knobelsdorff's severe
Corinthian colonnade under the dome, but the music room is done in
the perfectly accomplished Rococo of Johann Michael Hoppenhaupt.
The stylistic varieties of Potsdam expose very clearly the restlessness of
the 'forties – a restlessness beginning to be felt in all countries and
which was only to be resolved in the renewed interest in theoretical
principle in the next decade.

Palace-building, obviously, is part of the dynastic history of Europe
and it follows that in countries where dynastic questions had been
pretty well settled palaces were not built. Blenheim Palace is a freak
which, in its very character as a gift to a national hero on the part of a
Queen who built no palaces herself, underlines the truth of this for
England. In France after Louis XIV, palace-building was a meaningless proposition and the accumulated talent of French architecture

27, 28, 29 Russia had relied on foreign architects ever since the Middle Ages, and with
Peter the Great's ambition to modernize his empire, that reliance became even
stronger. Below left: Peterhof, by a Frenchman, Jean-Baptiste Leblond, 1716–17.
Peter's daughter Elizabeth turned to the Italian Bartolomeo Rastrelli, who built the
palace of Tsarskoe Selo (below right) and the Winter Palace in St Petersburg
(opposite), and partly remodelled Peterhof, all in the 1740s and 50s. These Russian
Baroque palaces are notable for their masterful handling of very long façades and for
their use of exterior colour, a resource that had been comparatively neglected in
Central and Southern Europe.

sought outlets elsewhere. De Cotte and Boffrand were constantly in request at foreign courts. Boffrand, as we have seen, participated at Würzburg and his major works were the palaces for Leopold, Duke of Lorraine, at Nancy and Lunéville, with the same Duke's country house called La Malgrange. The last two were never finished; neither was the palace he began for the Elector Max Emanuel of Bavaria near Brussels.

In Russia, under Peter I and his successors, the opportunities for immigrant architects were considerable. The first celebrity whom Peter drew to his new capital at St Petersburg was Schlüter, anxious for employment after the collapse of his Berlin tower. But Schlüter shortly died and Peter fared little better with the distinguished

Frenchman Leblond, who did, however, live long enough to provide the design for Peterhof and to train the first Russian-born architect to practice in a full classical idiom, Zemtsov. But it was under Peter's daughter, Elizabeth Petrovna, and her architect, Bartolommeo Francesco Rastrelli, that Russian Baroque architecture emerged as something with a character of its own. Rastrelli was the son of an Italian sculptor who had come to St Petersburg with Leblond and had thus been in Russia since the age of fifteen. He was sent to Paris to study under de Cotte, saw something of Germany and Italy and returned with a markedly Rococo taste. In the ten-year reign of Anna Joannovna he was set to reconstruct the Winter Palace as it then stood (the work of two obscure Italians) but his real opportunities came with the accession of Elizabeth in 1740. For her he completed the Summer Palace – a timber work, long since destroyed – proceeded to the Anichkov Palace (also destroyed), a gay, lofty building with a Baroque version of Russian domes on the pavilions, then reconstruct-ed Leblond's Peterhof, doubling its length, and finally engaged on the total rebuilding both of the Great Palace at Tsarskoe Selo and of the Winter Palace at St Petersburg. In the last three of these Rastrelli had to cope with façades of preposterous length (that bitter legacy of Versailles). He divided them pavilion-wise and applied classical orders in quantity. At Tsarskoe Selo a lumpish Corinthian parades in three different heights; at the Winter Palace the Corinthian, fantastically elongated, balances over an Ionic and carries statues on pedestals at top, giving a sense of forced theatricality, a brutally literal Bibiena stage-design. Anywhere in Western Europe this would have been intolerable. In the tremendous water-girt flatness of St Petersburg it achieved what was needed, an effect of absolute, grim and careless dominion.

Rastrelli's palaces came later in the Baroque season; the Winter Palace was finished only in 1762. But, strangely, the last triumphant expression of the palace theme was in the country of so many of its sources – Italy. In the earlier part of the century there had been little

30 The Stupinigi, 1714–33, was built as a hunting-lodge outside the Piedmontese capital of Turin, but its splendour belies such a humble purpose. Filippo Juvarra's plan radiates from the star-shaped central hall whose architecture dissolves into painted mythology on a lavish scale.

31, 32 Caserta, near Naples, 1751–74, is one of the largest palaces in Europe, designed to give the Bourbons of Naples the same prestige as those of France. Its architect, Luigi Vanvitelli, did not avoid monotony in its long façade, but the plan combines rationality with some spectacular set-pieces. The staircase shown in pl. 9 is near centre on the right.

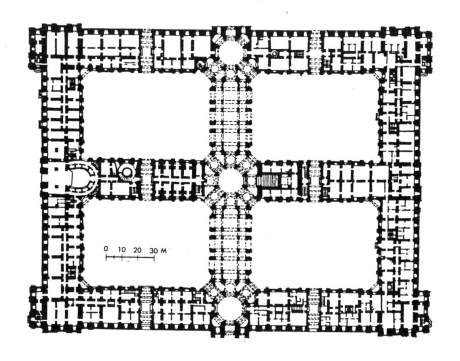

occasion for palace-building. At Turin, indeed, the capital of the newly created Kingdom of Savoy, Filippo Juvarra brought French and Italian influences together in the Palazzo Madama and that tour-de-force in radial planning, the castle of Stupinigi, built in 1729–33. And from Turin, Juvarra gave the plans for the palaces of Mafra for John V of Portugal and of Madrid for Philip V of Spain. But the last episode in our story takes place at Naples.

Naples, after 230 years of delegated rule, obtained a dynasty of her own with the ascent to the throne in 1734 of the Bourbon Charles III. Twenty-five years of enlightened despotism followed, with Charles entrenching his power on the classic model of his forbear Louis XIV. The creation of a Neapolitan Versailles was predictable and it was for this that he called Luigi Vanvitelli from Rome in 1751. Between that year and 1774 the palace of Caserta was built. It is famous for its size. There are said to be 1,200 rooms and the rigid lines of the lay-out stretch over the countryside as far as the eye can reach. But Caserta is not really on the Versailles model. Its plan – a cross within a rectangle providing four huge and identical inner courts – has something of the character of the Escorial and earlier 'ideal' plans for the Renaissance. In the architectural treatment, certainly, French classicism is thoroughly reflected but in the monumental parts of the interior there is something different again – a contrivance (arising from the plan) of dramatic Baroque perspectives which remind one of Piranesi. Caserta is a splendid fusion, on Italian soil, of Italian and French skills, addressed to the palace problem in the last years when that problem could still be taken with immense seriousness and at unlimited expense.

CHAPTER THREE

The Demonstrations of Faith

Now let us go back to our datum of 1700 and consider religious architecture as it developed from 1700 up to the mid-century. There is an obvious and very meaningful division here between the Catholic and Protestant worlds of the 18th century, a division which, one feels, ought to be reflected in obvious distinctions of plan and style in their respective religious buildings. It is, indeed, so reflected but with all sorts of subtle and intriguing distortions. As a wide generalization it is fair to say that high Baroque adventure belongs to the Catholic world and restrained classicism to the Protestant. Yet in London, under Anne, distinctly Baroque churches were being designed, while one of the first churches north of the Alps to have a classically Roman portico was the imperial Karlskirche in Vienna, begun by Fischer von Erlach in 1716. If, by a little special pleading, one claims for the dome of St Paul's in London (finished 1709) a Protestant-classical sobriety, what Catholic element is discoverable in the still more restrained, more classical dome of Ste Geneviève, Paris (now the Panthéon), deriving from St Paul's fifty years later? The truth is, of course, that on the Protestant side, by 1700, the need for a distinctive architectural attitude had in most (though not all) parts of Europe somewhat faded. In England, both Inigo Jones and Wren had, long since, made their Protestant statements – Jones in his Tuscan temple at Covent Garden (1630) and Wren in his galleried halls built after the London Fire of 1666. In Holland, Hendrick de Keyser had produced his Greek-cross model (the Noorderkerk, Amsterdam) by 1620. In France, where Protestant architecture was to have no future, Salomon de Brosse had in 1623 proposed a noble prototype in the form of a basilica. Some of these were departures of enduring importance but their lasting effect was in plan-form rather than style.

33 In the Wieskirche, in Bavaria, by Dominikus Zimmermann, 1746–54, architecture of column and vault is firmly Baroque, but the Rococo magic has swept through it leaving the interior transfigured as if commemorating a moment of ecstasy.

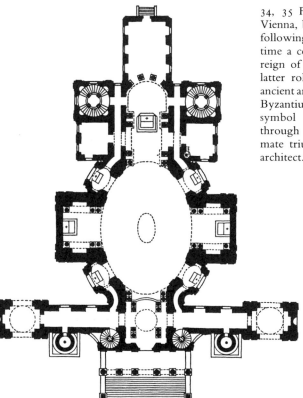

34, 35 Fischer von Erlach's Karlskirche, Vienna, begun 1716, was a votive church, following a plague epidemic, but at the same time a complex formal celebration of the reign of the Emperor Charles VI. In the latter role it brings together allusions to ancient and modern Rome and possibly also Byzantium and Paris; it is thus a collective symbol of architectural achievement through the ages, demonstrating the ultimate triumph of the Emperor – and his architect.

36 The Kollegienkirche in Salzburg, consecrated in 1707, by Fischer von Erlach, takes its basic vocabulary from Roman Baroque: but the high dome, the convex front between twin towers, and the crowning of the towers with carved pinnacles are products of Fischer's imagination. (From Fischer's *Entwurf einer historischen Architektur*.)

In the Catholic world there was no challenge to produce new types at a basic level. The challenge to Catholicism was of a different order – to reinforce and extend received traditions and to demonstrate with the utmost force the Church's transcendental role. This was the sanction of the Baroque as it had flourished in Rome under Urban VIII and his three successors – the Baroque of Bernini, Borromini and Cortona. This Baroque was not the art of the Counter-Reformation but the art of the situation which it brought about. It was an art with a wholly new function: nothing less than the immediate conveyance through the senses and by the rhetoric of the combined arts, of religious illumination. By 1700 this new function had been fully demonstrated in Italy. In the next half century it was demonstrated again and again in central Europe in performances of the utmost brilliance.

Catholicism in Central Europe

It is in Austria and Bohemia that we see the first of the new Baroque episodes and in both countries the way had been prepared by immigrant Italians. We have already observed how the works of

Bernini and Borromini inspired the palace builders. In church building they were no less a source of wonder and emulation. Bernini's oval church of S. Andrea al Quirinale in Rome is echoed time and again in transalpine plans. Borromini's little masterpiece S. Carlo alle Quattro Fontane, with its sense of instantaneity, of dramatically arrested motion,was perhaps the most compelling influence of all. We see its effect at once in Fischer von Erlach's churches in Salzburg, built at the end of the 17th century. We see it again in churches in Prague with which the name of Christoph Dientzenhofer is associated. At Gabel in northern Bohemia, Lucas von Hildebrandt, the architect of the Belvedere, introduced the 'three-dimensional arch' (curved in plan as well as in elevation) which Guarini, Borromini's Piedmontese follower, had made famous at S. Lorenzo in Turin and which was to travel far through central Europe. The originality and daring of these new interpretations of the Baroque are astonishing. Dientzenhofer especially, an illiterate mason of German origin, seized the Baroque ideas and handled them with all the authority of a Gothic master of two centuries earlier. Moreover, in his church of the Benedictines at Brunau, near Prague, he achieved that identity of architecture and fresco-painting which, deriving ultimately from S. Ignazio in Rome, runs through the whole of central European Baroque and is even more striking in church interiors than in the staircases and halls of the palaces.

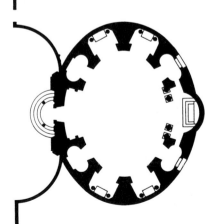
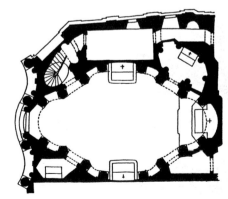

37, 38, 40 Two Roman Baroque plans and their Central European progeny. Opposite: S. Andrea al Quirinale by Bernini (see pl. 1) and S. Carlo alle Quattro Fontane by Borromini (see pl. 3). Below: the church of Gabel in Bohemia, by Lucas von Hildebrandt, its dome standing over 'three-dimensional' arches.

39 The church of Brunau (Břevnov), near Prague, 1708–15, by Christoph Dientzenhofer, uses a system of overlapping transverse ovals to give a sense of movement – a device which became a hallmark of the Dientzenhofer family.

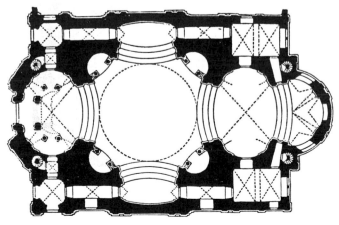

0   5   10 M.

41 For the medieval abbey church of Sedlec, Giovanni Santini designed in 1712 a new vault in a strange 'Gothic' style that seems to anticipate the Gothic Revival of Walpole and Wyatt later in the century.

42, 43, 44 Banz, central Germany: interior, exterior and plan. The Benedictine abbey was built by Johann Dientzenhofer between 1710 and 1718. The monastic orders were experiencing a phase of sudden affluence in Central Europe, leading to lavish rebuildings of churches and monastic buildings, including libraries (see pls. 126, 128). The plan of Banz contains the same system of interlocking ovals as Brunau.

Among minor masters of the period is the eccentric Giovanni Santini Aichel (usually called Santini), a native of Prague with an Italian grandfather, who had visited Holland and England as well as Italy. In him we have the curious spectacle of Bohemian Baroque adopting Gothic forms. His plans are Baroque of an advanced and original kind and the Gothic was probably adopted for picturesque or historical reasons. The pastiche Gothic vaults at Kladruby (1712) and Sedlec are part of the restorations and extensions of medieval churches.

From these beginnings in Austria and Bohemia the new church art spread into Franconia, Swabia, Switzerland, Bavaria and Saxony. Its carriers were the monastic orders. The monasteries of central Europe had, in the late 17th century, entered a period of considerable affluence. While their responsibilities, if anything, diminished, their

44

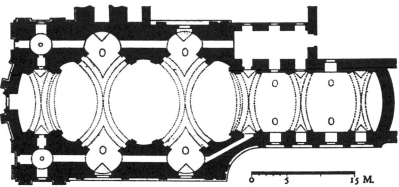

landed wealth increased and when ably administered they had much
the same potential for building enterprise as the greater nobility.
Countless Benedictine, Cistercian and Premonstratension houses
rebuilt themselves in whole or in part, often on a scale and with a
cumulative effect not inferior to great palaces. One conspicuous
palace-monastery Europe already had in Philip II's Escorial. The
greater monasteries of Austria and Germany are its later and far less
dour equivalents.

Leonard Dientzenhofer, a brother of Christoph, rebuilt the hill-
sited monastery of St Michael at Bamberg in 1696–1702 and that of
Schönthal in Württemberg in 1700–13. Another brother, Johann,
rebuilt in 1710–18 the monastery church at Banz, again on a
spectacular hilltop site over the Main. Here the Dientzenhofer genius

45

struck a new note. The nave vault is a system of interlaced ovals with differential emphasis at succeeding levels, so contrived that the physical vault seems to gape apart to reveal a heavenly vault where events from the Old and New Testament are depicted. On the one hand, here is a brilliant variation on a Borrominesque idea; but on the other a revival of that plastic ingenuity which belongs to Bohemian Gothic, a style for which the Dientzenhofers must have had a deep respect.

The Dientzenhofers were a family of working masons and it is characteristic of much of the monastic building of the period that the designers came from this artisan class and were not of the courtly type like Hildebrandt, whose education was theoretical and connected with military affairs. Thus, at the great Benedictine monastery of Melk, towering over the Danube, the presiding architect was Jakob Prandtauer, a sculptor-mason, neither travelled nor deeply read. He replanned the whole monastery on its old site, placing the church on an axis between converging wings, with its towered west end standing over a court which grows bastion-like from the rock. In such a building it becomes evident that an ambitious abbot could have not only the same resources but the same addiction as any prince to the sheer lust for architectural performance.

In Bavaria, monastic patronage ran parallel with the Court patronage of the Elector, Max Emanuel, mentioned in a previous section. Max Emanuel's triumph was to bring Effner and Cuvilliés to Munich and foster the creation of Bavarian Rococo. In church architecture, patronage was in the hands of Benedictine abbots, the great artistic personalities being the brothers Cosmas Damian Asam and Egid Quirin Asam. Sons of a successful fresco painter, both had been sent under episcopal patronage to Rome. Cosmas Damian became a painter; Egid Quirin a sculptor. Both practised architecture. But the architecture of the Asams is of a kind which flows so immediately and equally into painting on the one hand and sculpture on the other as almost to be an art peculiar to itself. Cosmas Damian expressed the components of his art as *architectura: scenografia: decus*. *Scenografia* is the clue to much of it. His abbey church at Weltenburg, begun 1718, is on the lines of Bernini's S. Andrea al Quirinale but Bernini's swift motion is jerked to a halt, light is poured in from

45 The abbey of Melk, on a hill overlooking the Danube, was rebuilt by Jakob Prandtauer, 1702–14. With a true feeling for the picturesque, he brought the containing wall of the abbey to the furthest extremity of the rocky site and formed an arched opening as a visual link with the valley below: one of the most memorable groupings in Austrian Baroque.

mysterious sources and in a blaze of light behind the high altar a figure of St George on horseback rides into the church – Egid Quirin being, of course, the sculptor. Egid Quirin was also the creator of the astounding *tableau vivant* at nearby Rohr, where the whole scene of

47

46, 47 The two most dazzling displays of *scenographia* in Bavarian Baroque, both by the Asam brothers: Röhr (above), with the Assumption of the Virgin rendered with the utmost realism, and Weltenburg (opposite), with St George caught in the act of slaying his dragon.

the Assumption is as it were photographically caught and rendered into an awe-inspiring sculptural group. Egid Quirin, in later years (1733–46), built in Munich at his own cost and next to his own house a church dedicated to the then lately canonized St John of Nepomuk. Its narrow front is a sculptor's fantasia on themes by Borromini; its interior is again a fantasia this time with reference to Bernini as well. But these Romans are left standing, as the Bavarian sculptor dissolves their attributes into his own swift theatrical invention.

The brilliant Asams were in request far and wide, often installing their effects in the churches of other architects. Among their Bavarian contemporaries was another pair of brothers, a trifle older and remarkably different – Dominikus and Johann Baptist Zimmermann. Dominikus began as a working mason but rose to be an architect under Premonstratensian patronage. Johann Baptist was a painter and plasterer who acquired a reputation through his association with Cuvilliès at the Amalienburg. The two Zimmermanns together brought the Rococo of the Court into church architecture, converting it, in the process, into something far less sophisticated and, in fact, initiating the 'Bavarian style' echoed in so many hundreds of country churches. Their first important work was the oval pilgrimage church at Steinhausen, built in 1728–31, the very antithesis, with its quaint curly forms, of the Baroque sophistication of the Asams. But their triumph came fifteen years later in the pilgrimage church of Die Wies. Here, within a barn-like outer shell an oval dome rises from sturdy, angular pairs of shafts attached by arches to the walls. It is simple. But through the peasant simplicity blows a Rococo of fresh, almost naive invention, distributing its effects with unerring precision and lifting the peasant barn to a paradisiac level.

But the climax of monastic building in central Europe came when, under Cistercian patronage, Balthasar Neumann undertook the pilgrimage church of Vierzehnheiligen in 1743 and, under Benedictine patronage, the abbey church of Neresheim in 1747. Neumann was now, in his late fifties, the most brilliant figure in European architecture, with all the technical proficiency of the French school and a complete mastery of the innovations of the Bohemian and Austrian. Vierzehnheiligen stands superbly over the Main valley, with Banz, built by Johann Dientzenhofer thirty-three years earlier, on the

48, 49 The church of St Johannes Nepomuk in Munich was built by the Asam brothers next to their own house and at their own expense, 1733–46. The façade, with its concave-convex-concave rhythm and theatrical sculpture, screens an interior where all the arts combine to produce a stunning impact. Above the cornice, mysteriously lit, the three persons of the Trinity are realistically interpreted in a dazzling combination of painting and sculpture.

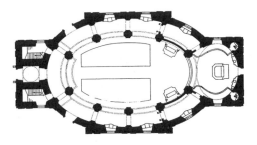

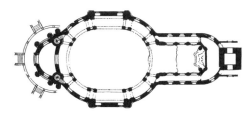

50, 51, 52 Two churches by Dominikus Zimmermann, both using the oval plan: Steinhausen (top) and the Wies (above and below). The pilgrimage church 'an die Wies'(literally,'in the meadow') was built as the setting for a miraculous image. The use of stucco enables the architect to do the apparently impossible (e.g. inverted arches), while progression through space is echoed in a chromatic progression. The white nave leads to a sanctuary where the colour deepens to blue and red.

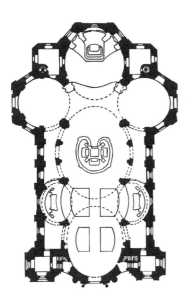

53, 54, 55 Vierzehnheiligen is another pilgrimage church, by Balthasar Neumann, 1743–72, and the most sophisticated of all the churches based on an oval. The plan consists, indeed, of five ovals, the largest forming the nave which contains the shrine of the 'Fourteen Saints'.

opposite bank. The shape of Banz, we have seen, was based on a scheme of intersecting ovals. So is that of Vierzehnheiligen, but there the play of ovals is more elaborate and reaches a result which is not only more dramatic but, in its swaying continuity, exactly expressive of the church's double purpose – to embrace, centrally, a pilgrim shrine, while still culminating in a high altar. Neresheim, in the Swabian alps, demanded a simpler solution and is therefore less complex, less mobile; it expresses with monumental felicity the conclusion of the Baroque story in central Europe.

A twist to classicism: Italy and France

During the first half of the century there is little else in Catholic Europe to approach the church-building achievements of the Dientzenhofers and Neumann. In Rome, the most sensational episode of the period was the competition held in 1732 for the façade of S. Giovanni in Laterano. Twenty-three architects took part and the winner was Alessandro Galilei. His design is related to Maderna's west front of St Peter's but the arrangement of the columns is in a more classical spirit and, in fact, much in the spirit of what was being done by Wren and his circle in England. As Galilei had spent five years in England and been associated with Vanbrugh it is difficult to avoid the conclusion that the new trend of English classicism was a factor in his success. Whether or not that is so, the façade of the Lateran church is a pointer to a change in Italian Baroque taste – a feeling for articulation as against generalization and a new objectivity towards the antique. Something of the sort is seen also in Fuga's new façade of Sta Maria Maggiore of 1741–43.

In Piedmont a short but really noble period of achievement opened with the reign of Vittorio Amedeo II of Savoy, who invited Filippo Juvarra, then at the height of his reputation, to enter his service. The result was a vast programme of palace-building, town-planning and church-building in and around Turin between 1714 and Juvarra's death in 1736. Two of the churches are among the most original of their time, for Juvarra, with all the experience and authority of the Italian tradition behind him, could still strike out inventions as daring as Neumann (his exact contemporary) on the other side of the Alps. At the Chiesa del Carmine in Turin (1732–35), for instance, he

56 The façade of S. Giovanni in Laterano, added to the Early Christian basilica after a competition held in 1732. The architect was Alessandro Galilei, and his design marks a return to orthodox classicism after the liberation of the Baroque. The influence of Vanbrugh is possible, since Galilei had spent some time in England and been consulted by one of Vanbrugh's clients.

57 Chiesa del Carmine, Turin, by Filippo Juvarra, 1732–35. In a generally conventional plan and elevation, Juvarra intrudes an exciting innovation, the piers being linked by 'bridges' forming a continuous gallery with chapels beneath.

substituted for the traditional basilican section a section more nearly that of a northern 'hall' church with each aisle bay containing a chapel below and a gallery above, Gothic in essence but handled with faultless Baroque technique. High above the plain of Turin is Juvarra's masterpiece, the mountain sanctuary built by Vittorio Amedeo as a thank-offering to the Virgin – the Superga. This, built in 1717–31, consists of a rectangular monastery building from which projects a circular church carried upwards into a dome and forwards into a deep vaulted portico: no Gothic here but a wonderful new synthesis of Renaissance and Baroque experience.

Also in Piedmont, the genius of Bernardo Vittone sparkles with modest brilliance in his many small-town churches. A generation younger than Juvarra, he combined some of that master's improvisations with the geometrical inventions of Guarini, especially the vertical perspective of dome seen through dome, creating a celestial illusion of space beyond space. In the little central-space church at Vallinotto, near Carignano, the lower dome is a network of ribs; above this comes a painted dome with an *oculus*, through which a second painted dome is seen, and finally, visible through a second, smaller *oculus*, the brilliantly lit lantern which surmounts the whole.

Moving from Italy to France we again find that church-building is in no way comparable, either in patronage or performance, to that of central Europe. In France, as in Austria and Germany, there were indeed wealthy monasteries which employed their revenues in grandiose reconstructions by the best architects: the great Robert de Cotte, for instance, rebuilt the monastery of St Denis, as well as the episcopal palaces of Toulouse and Strasbourg (now used respectively as a town-hall and a museum). But France had moved too far from the Middle Ages to share that extraordinary union of spirituality and wilful extravagance which gave us churches like Ottobeuren, Vierzehnheiligen and Die Wies. The characteristic and significant product of 18th-century France is the new façade added to an existing church, a façade being a conspicuous and often costly gesture towards religion rather than a religious act. Such an attitude, in the age of Voltaire, is predictable. Most of these façades are based on Italian or Mansartian prototypes but it happens that one of them – that of St Sulpice, Paris – was a monument of considerable originality and

58 Juvarra's church of the Superga, 1717–31, crowns a hill outside Turin. A simple diagram of cubes and cylinders is the basis for a majestic exercise in classical technique, to which the spreading balustraded platform adds immense dignity.

59 The dome of Vallinotto, a tiny village church by Bernardo Vittone in Piedmont. The inspiration is clearly Guarini's dome of S. Lorenzo in Turin (pl. 4), with even more interpenetrating ribs and light sources.

60 West front of St Sulpice in Paris, begun in 1733 by the French-Italian architect Servandoni. Here was a break-away from the Baroque, evidently inspired by English influences, for the first version, subsequently modified, was based on the west front of St Paul's. Of the two towers, that on the north (left) is from Servandoni's design, that on the south is by Chalgrin, 1777.

influence. The architect here was J. N. Servandoni, a Florentine by birth with an anonymous French father, and he won the commission in a competition of 1732 – the very year, as it happens, of the competition for the new façade of S. Giovanni Laterano in Rome. By a further coincidence, Servandoni's façade, like Galilei's, was affected by English influence and was in its first version a paraphrase of the west front of St Paul's. In execution, however, it was greatly modified and its success has less to do with Wren than with Servandoni's concern to exhibit a grandiose and loyal interpretation of the Roman orders.

An intellectual thread of a different kind runs through some French church-building, arising from a lively but totally unromantic concern with Gothic. Louis XIV himself had dictated Gothic for the new west front of Ste Croix, Orléans, in 1709; but this was a grand irrelevance, for the new thought turned on the interpretation of Gothic ideas in classical language. There are, here and there, churches with immensely elongated classical columns supporting thin Roman vaults or domes. The most breathtaking of these is Nicolas Nicole's church of the Madeleine at Besançon, where a soaring Gothic effect is obtained

61 At the church of the Madeleine in Besançon, Nicolas Nicole built what is structurally a Gothic church but with piers formed of classically correct pairs of Ionic columns.

with the minimum of distortion in the classical elements. The integration of Classical and Gothic principles had become, by the middle of the century, an important aspect of emergent Neo-classicism. In the church of Ste Geneviève, Paris, later to become secularized as the Panthéon, it reaches a climax. The church was designed for Louis XV by Jacques Germain Soufflot in 1757–58, by which time the ideas of Cordemoy had been taken over and effectively propagated by Laugier. At Ste Geneviève, Soufflot attempted and very nearly achieved Laugier's ideal of a classical building of the utmost purity which nevertheless embodies the structural integrity of a vaulted Gothic cathedral. It is the first great church of the 18th century to stand completely outside the Baroque.

Spain, Portugal and Latin America

It is perhaps characteristic of 18th-century France that while in general there was no great incentive towards church-building, some of the churches built had a high philosophical, innovating importance. In Spain, on the other hand, the cultural bankruptcy reached under the

59

62, 63, 64 The church of Ste Geneviève, now the Panthéon, in Paris, begun in 1757 by J. G. Soufflot, was a more radical attempt to adapt classical elements to Gothic structure, i.e. a cruciform building supported on a system of balancing thrusts and counterthrusts. Stylistically it is severely classical, including a central dome and a huge western portico. Soufflot, however, miscalculated the stresses, and his ample windows, seen in the engraving, c. 1790, had to be filled in.

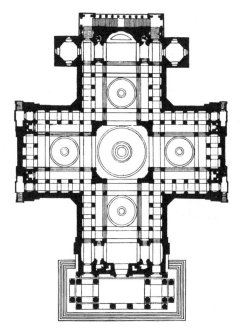

last Habsburgs continued into the century of Bourbon rule. What distinguishes church architecture in Spain under Philip V is a violent intensification of some of the more neurotic aspects of Italian Mannerism, especially the destruction of conventional forms by a coruscation of ornamental detail. The naïve desire to produce amazement in the mind of the observer by leaving no surface, no edge undistorted is found in Germany but never with the same obsessional completeness as in the works associated with the Churriguera family in Spain. José de Churriguera, who died in 1725, was the most eminent but it was his brothers, his children and his followers who pushed the style to its most shocking extremes – in such works, for instance, as the sacristy of the Carthusian monastery at Granada, begun by Luis de Arévalo in 1727. This kind of puzzle-work has a connection with

65 Spanish Baroque remained relatively unadventurous spatially, but occasionally succumbed to a frenzy of ornament in which every architectural element – pilasters, capitals, cornices, window-surrounds – is broken into a mass of sharp edges and thick scrolls. Below: the sacristy of the Charterhouse of Granada, by Luis de Arévalo.

66 The *trasparente* of Toledo Cathedral, completed 1732 by Narciso Tomé, is difficult to convey photographically. It is essentially a screen, one side forming the back of the high altar, the other (seen here) visible from the ambulatory. Above it, one of the vaulting bays is removed and the opening is surrounded by figures of angels, Christ and the prophets enthroned on clouds.

67 Right: The west front of the cathedral of Santiago de Compostela, 1738–49, incorporates the square towers of the old Romanesque building but conceals them behind an exuberant display of decoration: the architect was F. de Casas y Novoa.

Spain's own complicated 'Plateresque' style of the 16th century. It has been suggested that its bizarre character may have been reinforced by acquaintance with the ancient art of Mexico but apart from the perpetual zig-zagging of cornices there is little to support this idea; and Arévalo's decomposed pilasters at Granada are not all that much stranger than those given in the etchings of Wendel Dietterlin published at Nuremberg in 1594–98 and very widely circulated. In short, the Churrigueresque is something of a throw-back, perhaps nostalgically to Spain's age of glory. More easily linked with contemporary practice elsewhere is the art of the *trasparente*, of which the greatest Spanish example, in Toledo Cathedral, is probably the most effective in the world, more surprising even than the Asams'

performance in Bavaria. Designed to honour the Sacrament and as a protest against the Jansenist heresy it consists of a flood-lit altarpiece in high relief for which the source of light – a chamber over a dismembered and disguised Gothic vault – itself contains a heavenly vision. Completed by Narciso Tomé in 1732, it conveys, as so much of the architecture of Spain does convey, an intensity of feeling overriding any deep concern with architectural form.

One of the most spectacular pieces of 18th-century Spanish architecture and one in which the retrospective element comes out strongly is the main façade of Santiago de Compostella Cathedral, built in 1738–49. To maintain its prestige as a pilgrimage centre, the cathedral had, in 1650, been set on a course of restoration and

68 Santuario de Ocotlan, near Tlaxcala, Mexico. Between plain brick towers, the centre of the façade is as ornately modelled as the retable of an altar, magnified to a giant scale. By a strange coincidence of history, late Spanish Baroque had evolved to a point where it shared some characteristics of native Mexican architecture.

embellishment. It passed through the hands of three architects, all of whom worked in a style deriving from German or Flemish work of the previous century. Fernando de Casas, the designer of most of the west front, intensified the characteristics of the style in a composition of endless elaboration, with a multiplication of niches, scrolls, columns and broken pediments reminiscent of Dietterlin at his most explosive. This deliberate looking-back in church-building is emphasized when we reflect that the work is exactly contemporary with Filippo Juvarra's late Baroque façades at La Granja and Sacchetti's at the Royal Palace of Madrid.

Something must be said of the flood of Baroque church-building which the Spaniards released in those parts of the New World which they brought under their dominion. The conquest of the Americas was a joint adventure of state and church and as new towns arose so did their cathedrals. The religious orders followed with their convents and missions. Most of the cathedrals and greater churches were built between 1570 and 1650; the 18th century, which is our sole concern here, saw only the last phase. After the accession of Charles III in 1759, wealth and enterprise, touched by the spirit of European Enlightenment, were turning from church-building to the provision of universities, libraries and hospitals.

The typical Spanish–American cathedral of the late 17th century was a three-aisle barrel-vaulted structure with a domed crossing. At the west end stood two sturdy bell-towers with, between them, a 'retable façade' often of extreme elaboration. In Mexico the massive character of these buildings began to yield, early in the 18th century, to a more elegant type, first seen in the Capilla de los Reyes (1718–37) in Mexico cathedral and subsequently on a larger scale in a number of Mexican churches of which the most celebrated is the Santuario de Ocotlan near Tlaxcala, some hundred miles from Mexico City. The western towers shoot up to twice the height of the nave, their lower parts quite bare, the upper stages richly modelled with ornament

69 Jesuit mission at Concepción, Bolivia. The primitive character of such buildings as this erected by Spanish missionary priests in the settlements they created in South America, was dictated by local conditions. No connection with the speculative primitivism of Laugier need be sought.

partly of Churrigueresque character. Between the towers the 'retable' façade is dramatically intensified. In the highland provinces of Peru and Bolivia, the so-called '*mestizo*' style developed, a 'half-breed' style, in which recognizably Baroque elements are submerged in a wealth of ornamental carving with a strong native inflection.

Before leaving the Spanish possessions it is worth turning from the cathedrals to the humbler architectural performances of the Jesuit missions, especially in Paraguay, among the Guarani Indians. Here a strict rule of community life was laid down by the Jesuit Provincial, Diego de Torres, early in the 17th century, controlling dress, housing and routines of work, play and rest – a kind of Christian communism. These settlements or 'reductions' often turned out to be successful commercial enterprises but the conditions in which they worked, in tropical forests, dictated a primitive type of construction – sheds on wooden pillars with 'curtain-walling' in adobe. After *c*.1675 stone enclosures were introduced, and masonry vaulting from about 1725, but the building of timber churches continued even after 1767, at which date the Jesuit order was expelled from America. Few of the timber buildings survive but the church at Yaguaron (1761–84) is representative. It is a prototypal temple such as might have sprung to the mind of a rational philosopher like Laugier, but the building's character arises in fact from a combination of European carpentry practice and native craftsmanship.

The history of Portuguese architecture in the 18th century differs considerably from that of Spain. The discovery of Brazilian gold in 1693 made the court of John V one of the most lavish in Europe. Architecturally, his reign is dominated by the building of the palace monastery of Mafra, an equivalent of the Escorial but with prime emphasis on the palace rather than the conventual element. It was the work of a German architect, J. F. Ludwig (known in Portugal as João Frederico Ludovice), who had served in the Imperial army and then worked under Andrea Pozzo in Rome. The influences of Bernini, Borromini and Fontana are evident. The other great architect in 18th-century Portugal was an Italian, Niccolo Nazzoni (Nasoni). His most important work in Portugal was the oval church of São Pedro dos Clérigos at Oporto. Thus, Portuguese architecture in the 18th century was dominated by Italian and central European influences in a way

70, 71 The vast palace-monastery of Mafra, north of Lisbon, 1717–30, by the German architect Ludwig (or Ludovice) was Portugal's answer to the Escorial. The church, with its two-towered façade and domed interior, forms the centre of the main range.

72 Church of São João d'el Rei at Sâo Francisco in the Portuguese colony of Brazil. Designed by Portuguese architects in 1774, it is unaffected by its transatlantic environment and the use of local materials.

that Spain was not; Baroque passed to Rococo and Giovanni Carlo Bibiena designed the Memoria Church at Belem near Lisbon in 1760. After Lisbon was destroyed by an earthquake in 1755, the new city arose in Neo-classical formality, the rebuilt churches, however, retaining much of the Rococo.

In Brazil, the church architecture was more closely associated with that of the mother country than was the case in Mexico and Peru with Spain. The church of São João d'El Rei at São Francisco is a typical example of Portuguese Rococo, designed in 1774 by the Portuguese architects A. F. Lisboa and F. de Lima Cerqueira, and loyally executed in the materials of the new environment, materials often more sympathetic to refined detail than the hard granite of Portugal.

The Protestant world

It will be seen that the history of Catholic religious art in the 18th century flows in a great tide from Italy through central Europe, with eddies and pools in France and Spain – Italy herself, the source of it all, lapsing into relative calm. The Protestant world suggests a different image – local fountains of endeavour, rising and subsiding in circumstances of varied kinds. Protestant churches were built less for the glorification of God than for the accommodation of his worshipping servants and in most Protestant countries such accommodation was amply supplied by the thousands of churches standing over from pre-Reformation days – their architectural splendours reduced rather than amplified. There was no incentive to rebuild such churches – unless, indeed, they collapsed or were burnt down. Outside such (not infrequent) contingencies the only good reason for building a church was that a congregation required it. Typical circumstances in which this might happen were rapid urban expansion or the incursion of a tolerated Protestant population in a predominantly Catholic nation.

After 1700, England undoubtedly takes first place as a Protestant church-building nation. The Great Fire of London of 1666 had produced a crisis which involved not only the total rebuilding of a great metropolitan cathedral (St Paul's) but the construction of more than fifty new parish churches. By 1700 the work of reconstruction was virtually complete but in 1710 a change of ministers under Queen

Anne brought about a state-patronized church-building movement, again in London but this time with the purpose of replenishing church accommodation in the rapidly expanding suburbs. In this new movement, the leading figure was Nicholas Hawksmoor and his six churches built under the Act of 1711 constitute an episode of singular originality and power. Much in Hawksmoor is taken from his master, Sir Christopher Wren, the genius of the post-fire reconstruction; but he had a strongly marked personal style, a feeling for the Roman Baroque, and an intense interest both in the more recondite areas of antiquity and in the architecture of the Middle Ages. He could combine, in Christ Church, Spitalfields, 1714–29, a Gothic broach spire with a Roman Doric portico. In another church, St Anne, Limehouse, the lantern on the tower can be read either as a paraphrase of the Gothic lantern of St Botolph's, Boston, Lincolnshire, or as a romantic reconstruction of the Athenian 'tower of the winds'.

Another English architect, whose ultimate influence in the whole English-speaking world can hardly be overestimated, was James Gibbs. He was almost the only one of his generation who had been to Rome and his first church, St Mary-le-Strand, London (built 1714–17 under the Act mentioned above), reflects his studies under Carlo Fontana. It looks like a Catholic church and we know, in fact, that Gibbs was a secret adherent to the old faith. The church was severely criticized and Gibbs's later masterpiece, the church of St Martin-in-the-Fields (1721–26) shows a very different approach. With its great Roman portico and its steeple in the style of Wren, it was accepted at once as a model church for Anglican worship. It was imitated throughout the British Isles, in the American Colonies, in India and eventually even in Australia.

It might be thought that so powerful and well established a school of church-building as the English would find imitators in Protestant countries on the Continent but apart from a few Wren-like steeples (that of the Sophienkirche in Berlin, 1729–35, is a good example) this was not the case. English churches tended to be built on the old nave-and-aisles model, often with a short chancel. Both Lutheran and Reformed congregations showed a marked preference for the central space idea as demonstrated in the 17th-century churches of Amsterdam and Haarlem and Johan de la Vallée's impressive derivative at

73, 74, 75 In Protestant England, the classical tradition of Inigo Jones and Wren was periodically subject to Baroque influence; but 'English Baroque' includes buildings of a kind to which 'Baroque' is only applied for want of a more explicit term. This applies especially to the churches of Hawksmoor, grand architectural gestures which combine ideas from the antique with elements from the English Middle Ages. Above: the steeples of Christ Church, Spitalfields, and St Anne's, Limehouse, built between 1714 and 1730. Left: St Mary-le-Strand, London, 1714–17, by James Gibbs, is a church in which Baroque influence is unambiguous. Gibbs had studied under Carlo Fontana in Rome.

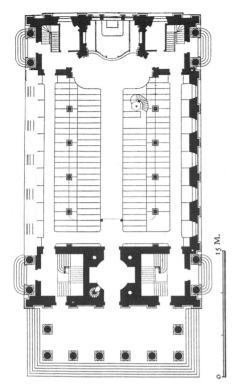

76, 77 In Gibbs' later church of St Martin-in-the-Fields, London, 1721–26, the Baroque spirit has fled and we have a sober classical temple with a Wren-like steeple penetrating the roof: a much criticised arrangement which, nevertheless, found favour throughout the English-speaking world.

78 St John's, Smith Square, 1714–28, by Thomas Archer, is one of the very few English churches to display exact knowledge of Roman Baroque. Its towers are demonstrably Borrominesque.

79, 80, 81 The Frauenkirche, Dresden, was begun in 1722 to the designs of Georg Bähr, an artisan-architect who began as a carpenter. He produced a centrally planned church with enormously tall windows, and slim piers leading up to a huge dome and lantern, with four corner turrets. The dome dominated the skyline of Dresden till its destruction in the air-raid of 1945. The interior was equally dramatic; the seats were arranged in tiers, like the circles of an opera-house, giving an uninterrupted view of the central pulpit.

Stockholm, the Katarinakyrka of 1656. In Silesia, where, in 1707, the Protestant population was permitted to build churches, they are on the Greek cross plan of this Stockholm example, dictated by the patronage of Charles XII. The central space preoccupation led eventually to the one really powerful Protestant church, outside England, of the first half of the century – the Frauenkirche at Dresden. This was commissioned by the civic authorities of Dresden, designed by the city architect, George Bähr, and built in 1725–43 with the express intention of rivalling the splendours of the neighbouring Court of the Elector Augustus. It combined a bold handling of the central space idea with Baroque sensationalism of a high order. Out of a square body rose an immense and steep masonry dome, dangerously supported within on a ring of eight arches between whose piers galleries mounted like those of a theatre. From the corners of the square, delicate spirelets ascended against the dome. In the skyline of Dresden the church struck an attitude as fantastic in its way as the Zwinger. Its total loss in the war was tragic.

After the middle of the 18th century, the history of church-building in Europe, whether Catholic or Protestant, has no density or effective continuity. In every country, late 18th-century churches tend to be one of two things: either tired stragglers from an old and exhausted tradition or else surprising and even enthralling adventures undertaken in the larger context of the new architectural theories. What those theories were and the extent to which they established a norm by which all buildings, including churches, can be judged is the matter to which we must now turn.

CHAPTER FOUR

A Plurality of Styles

Until comparatively recently, the architecture of Europe after the middle of the 18th century was characterized as belonging to 'the age of revivals'. This prolonged the 19th-century notion that every age should have its *style* and that there was, somehow, something wrong with an age which had no style of its own but was obliged to borrow from another. It was not seen that the reproduction of an old style may be just as significant and 'historical' an act as the creation of a new one and may reflect a profound alteration of attitude to other things than styles. This was the case in the period with which we are concerned. The changes which became manifest in the arts about the year 1750 have less to do with style than with the complete reorientation of European man to his historic past.

Revivalism in architecture was hardly new. For three hundred years the architecture of the Roman world had been the basis of all legitimate endeavour. Roman values, in the way in which they were interpreted, were considered absolute. But this position was inherently unstable. Attachment to classical culture meant attachment to history and attachment to history meant the remorseless widening of horizons in every direction until the uniqueness of Rome began to dissolve in a more general and immensely more complex vision of the whole European past. By 1750, students of the antique had come to realize the priority and anticipate the artistic precedence of Greek art. With the extension of travel and the beginnings of practical archaeology the varieties of style within the Roman world itself stood revealed. Furthermore, students of medieval history were beginning to appreciate the seriousness of intention, if not yet the formal values, of Gothic.

82 York Assembly Rooms, by Lord Burlington, represent a selfconscious return to antique formulae. The design was based on the so-called 'Egyptian Hall' as described by Vitruvius and interpreted by Palladio.

At the heart of the new situation was the displacement of a belief in one authority – Rome – by the conviction that there were, or could be, a plurality of authorities – Roman, Greek, Gothic and, for that matter, Chinese and Indian. A plurality leads at once to the possibility of choice and, in this case, to stylistic eclecticism. This or that style can be explored and exploited. This style can be combined with that style. And, most important of all, once the comparative study of historic styles is allowed to be legitimate, there is the irresistible analogue of a *new style*. This may be conceived as a personal style, a national style or simply as a rational abstraction from all styles. The way is clear for architectural revolution in a profound sense.

The word habitually employed for the architecture arising from this situation is 'Neo-classical'. This is misleading in so far as it seems to stress the archaeological and revivalist elements at the expense of the profounder philosophical and aesthetic character of the movement. Nevertheless, archaeology is of prime importance; indeed, the whole process of reorientation hinges upon it.

Systematic archaeological enquiry, as a development from the mere finding and collecting of antiquities, belongs to the mid-18th century. A landmark was the publication of the first volume of the Comte de Caylus' *Recueil des Antiquités* in 1752. Winckelmann's *Gedanken über die Nachahmung der griechischen Werke* came in 1755. Both Caylus and Winckelmann believed in the superiority of Greek art, with its 'noble simplicity', over Roman. This was not the view of Piranesi, the architect-etcher, who nevertheless did as much as anybody to uncover and display the wealth of the ancient world. Piranesi dedicated his genius to the pictorial reconstruction of Rome and the grandiose illustration of its ruins. His *Antichità Romane* belongs to 1748, his *Della Magnificenza*, championing the grandeur and variety of Rome against the promotion of the Greek, came in 1761.

The collection of new material from the Greek and Roman worlds proceeded during the same years. Excavations at Pompeii, under Bourbon patronage, were begun in 1748. These, however, aimed at the recovery of objects and paintings and the architecture of Pompeii had long to wait for recognition. The monuments of Athens were more rapidly put in circulation. The Frenchman J. D. Le Roy published *Les Ruines des plus beaux monuments de la Grèce* in 1758, to be followed four years later by the first volume of Stuart and Revett's *Antiquities of Athens*. Meanwhile, Robert Wood had led a party to Syria and published detailed records of Palmyra in 1753 and Baalbec in 1757. In 1764 came Robert Adam's survey of the Palace of Diocletian at Spalato (Split).

In this greatly widening vista of the classical past there was a bewildering choice which, while it had the effect of reducing the authority of the time-honoured interpreters of Rome – Serlio, Palladio, Scamozzi and even Vitruvius himself – provided no new directive for the future of architecture. A new directive, however, was already there in the rational propositions of Cordemoy and his later popularizer, Laugier, mentioned earlier in this essay. Laugier, in his image of the primitive hut as the prototype of all architectural splendour, was moving in the same direction as Winckelmann, with his ideal of 'noble simplicity' in painting and sculpture. Both Laugier and Winckelmann acknowledged the supremacy of Greece although neither, in their crucial publications, possessed any detailed information concerning Greek buildings or, indeed, authentic Greek sculpture. And even when Le Roy and Stuart and Revett had provided such information in their lavish folios it cannot be said that the impact on architecture was immediate. There was almost no literal imitation of Greek architecture on the Continent in the 18th century. There was a little more in England but the full 'Greek Revival' only commenced there after 1800.

'Noble simplicity'

The real nature of Neo-classicism in architecture is in a combination of the ideal of 'noble simplicity' with that of a rational application of the classical elements. With these ideals in their heads it was natural that architects should have continually before their eyes that ultimate image of nobility, simplicity and rationality which is the classical temple. To Laugier, the Maison Carrée at Nimes was the perfect building. Porticos, therefore, and colonnades of the strictest classical purity became essential attributes of churches and public buildings throughout Europe and it is these which have attracted such bored epithets as 'mere copyism' and 'cold imitation' to the Neo-classical movement. But in fact the spirit of the movement was far stronger

83, 84 The exploration of the past, first by artists and archaeologists, then by architects, began in earnest in the second half of the 18th century. The overpowering example of ancient Rome eventually gave way to that of Greece. Top: Piranesi's etching of the Arch of Constantine, from *Antichità Romane*, 1748. Bottom: the Propylaea of the Acropolis, Athens, from *Les Ruines des plus beaux monuments de la Grèce*, 1758, by J. D. Le Roy.

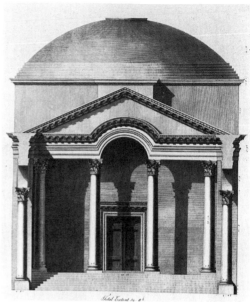

85, 86, 87 Top left: The Tower of the Winds, Athens, from *The Antiquities of Athens*, 1762–1816, by James Stuart and Nicholas Revett. Top right: the portico to the vestibulum from Robert Adam's *The Ruins of the Palace of the Emperor Diocletian at Spalato*, 1764. Bottom: view of the ruins of Baalbek from Robert Wood's *The Ruins of Balbec, otherwise Heliopolis in Coelosyria*, 1757.

than is evidenced by its specifically archaeologizing aspects. The very restriction to which architecture submitted induced a new sensitivity to exact statement, unbroken surfaces, broad mass and clear-cut space. These were capable, as Boullée, Ledoux and Soane were to demonstrate, of emotional expression of a new kind – an '*architecture parlante*' which made explicit the function of a building through its architectural elements.

A striking fact about Neo-classicism is its international character. The reason for this is that it was not the stylistic product of a school of architects in one country but rather an ideological movement to which individuals in several countries contributed and whose principles were easily communicable. Laugier was French, Winckelmann German, Piranesi Italian and the reputation of each was, almost from the first, international. The doctrine of Neo-classicism, being abstract and general, ran against national traditions and in fact had almost extinguished them by the end of the century, when the architecture of Europe attained a uniformity which held until the coming of romantic national revivals in the mid-19th century. It is significant that Neo-classicism had very little to do with Italy. Piranesi apart, no Italians made any substantial contribution. Italy was persistently scoured by the grand tourists and its monuments, by now regarded as an international heritage, recorded again and again by students – students who also presented their designs at the Italian academies and frequently carried off the prizes. If we try to discover the roots of the Neo-classical movement we shall not find them in Italy, nor indeed in France. The first categorical revolt against the Baroque and the first architectural statements of the new attitude are to be observed in England.

Something has already been said of the movement towards a rational interpretation of antiquity led by Colen Campbell in England from 1715. Campbell's own buildings rely to a great extent on Palladio and one of them, Mereworth in Kent, is externally an almost exact reproduction of the Villa Rotonda at Vicenza. To another house, the demolished Wanstead, he gave a Corinthian portico of the full dimensions appropriate to a Roman temple. A disciple of Campbell's was Richard Boyle, third Earl of Burlington. Burlington was both a powerful patron of the arts and himself a fastidious

88, 89 Two English Palladian houses by Colen Campbell. Top: Mereworth, Kent, 1723. Externally this is a copy of Palladio's Villa Rotonda at Vicenza, except that the dome of Mereworth is a little higher. Bottom: Wanstead, near London, 1715–20, with the dominant Corinthian portico claimed by Campbell as the first true temple portico in England.

90 Chiswick Villa, designed by Lord Burlington and attached to his family residence in 1725, takes the Villa Rotonda as a model but combines it with other, more recondite, sources.

designer. His own villa at Chiswick is a stylistic experiment introducing elements from Scamozzi, Palladio and the antique. A more daring experiment was the Assembly Rooms at York built in 1730 on the model of Palladio's reconstruction of the so-called 'Egyptian Hall'. Its classicism – which is to say its *Neo-classicism* – is totally uncompromising; it owes nothing to English tradition; it might have been built anywhere in Europe and at any time subsequent to its own and before, say, 1830.

Lord Burlington, with his friend and follower William Kent and a whole school of lesser men (James Gibbs being the only major architect not quite of their persuasion), succeeded in propagating his ideas to such an extent that English architecture up to 1760, at all levels from churches to farm-houses and common street-fronts, presents an amazing consistency. The movement and its products are generally designated 'Palladian', but it must not be forgotten how many other influences it embodies – from Scamozzi, from Inigo Jones, from antiquity (through Palladio's eyes) and even sometimes from Wren and the Baroque.

The question of the extent to which English architecture of this time influenced the Continent is a difficult one. It may be a coincidence that in the two great west-front competitions of 1732 – S. Giovanni in Laterano, Rome, and St Sulpice, Paris – the winning designs are more than suspect of containing English influence. In both cases, however, the influence would be from Wren and his school. Specific derivations from English Palladianism are rare. In France, the most obvious parallels are in the works of Jacques-Ange Gabriel. He was the son of Jacques Gabriel, whom he succeeded as *premier architecte* to Louis XV in 1742. In this office he built new wings flanking the entrance to Versailles, the Versailles Opéra, large additions to Compiègne and, in Paris, the Ecole Militaire and the two great palaces of the Place de la Concorde. Certainly, these designs move away from the exhausted style of Hardouin-Mansart towards calm and precise statement such as one associates with Palladianism. On the other hand the modelling is always strongly in the French tradition and the calmness is that of Perrault's east front of the Louvre. Perhaps the only building of Gabriel's in which there is a germ of English thought is the

91 Extension to Versailles by Jacques-Ange Gabriel – a self-contained block in the style of his buildings for the Place de la Concorde (pls. 164, 165) but ranging with the earlier work of Mansart, whose chapel is seen on the right.

92 Gabriel's Petit Trianon at Versailles, 1762–68, captures some of the English Palladians' severe dignity, but the delicacy of the modelling and the raised platform make it unmistakably French. Gabriel represents the conservative thread of French classicism, in contrast to his younger contemporaries, the 'revolutionary' architects Boullée and Ledoux.

Petit Trianon of Versailles. It is like a small Palladian country house, re-thought with all the expertise of French modelling and becoming in the end totally French.

Beyond Neo-classicism

The really important French departures in the direction of Neo-classicism had nothing to do with English Palladianism and were made by a few original thinkers against the background of French tradition reaching back to Lescot, Ducerceau and Philibert Delorme. One of these thinkers was J. G. Soufflot who, as we saw in the last section, undertook to build, in the Church of Ste Geneviève (now the Panthéon), a perfectly articulated vaulted structure in terms of the purest classicism. It was an attempt, nearly successful, to realize an ideal set forth by Laugier. Nothing of this structural audacity was attempted again. Experiment took a different form in the work of a younger architect, E. L. Boullée, whose Hôtel Brunoy, built in 1772, opposed all tradition by having a façade in the form of a classical propylaeum with arches between the columns. But in imagination

93 E. L. Boullée's design for a cenotaph for Sir Isaac Newton, 1784. In Boullée's drawings the Neo-classical imagination soars into a world of unbuildable abstractions. He believed that architecture should be based on 'nature', and 'nature' in an architectural context meant, for him, geometrical forms. His influence on the younger generation was extensive.

Boullée went much further than this. His executed works were few and his main contribution to Neo-classicism was in his theoretical writings and the astonishing series of designs made to accompany them. Boullée had been trained as a painter and conceived the idea that the full potentialities of architectural form could only be realized, at least for the time being, in graphic representations of buildings. His designs begin with classical compositions of impossible size but in due course he begins to strip away the classical attributes and present us with naked geometrical masses in dramatic relationships. The most celebrated of these abstract creations is the proposed Cenotaph for Isaac Newton, consisting of a sphere of something like 500 ft diameter, belted with cypress avenues and containing *space*, illuminated by stars, the latter contrived by minute penetrations in the surface. The tiny cenotaph itself rests at the bottom of the star-lit void.

Boullée might be dismissed as a superb freak if it were not for the fact that his influence counted for so much with the next generation. If we look through the published designs of those who carried off the Prix de Rome from their first publication in 1779 we find Boullée

85

94 The Barrière de la Villette, Paris, designed by C. N. Ledoux. The barrières were part of a scheme to enclose Paris with a new wall, solely for the purpose of collecting customs duties. In the hands of Ledoux, the barrières became temples and pavilions of funereal grandeur, combining an obsessive concern with geometrical forms and a somewhat grotesque taste in classical detail.

continually reflected and sometimes closely imitated. More important than this, Boullée was clearly the point of departure for one of the boldest innovators of the century – Claude Nicolas Ledoux.

Ledoux was born in 1736 and after a conventional training entered on a brilliant career as a designer of houses for the highest society, including one for Madame du Barry. Some of these houses have a rather English look but they are dramatically scaled and stress the hard edges of the volumes they contain. In 1771 he was appointed Inspector of the Royal Salt Works in the Franche-Comté and built the still partly surviving establishment at Arc-et-Senans (Chaux). By now he had developed an imaginative capacity as provocative and powerful as Piranesi's. Commissioned in 1784 to build the barrières (customs barriers) of Paris he proceeded on lines of such extravagance that he was dismissed. He narrowly escaped the guillotine and spent the rest of his life (he died in 1806) in following Boullée's example and expressing himself on paper.

Ledoux published his designs in a folio of 1804, sublimely entitled *l'Architecture Considérée sous le Rapport de l'Art, des Moeurs et de la Législation*. The book had been conceived long before and the designs probably belong mostly to the 'nineties. The importance of the book is two-fold. First, in the absolute freedom which Ledoux claims for architecture and the calibre of his own performances within that freedom. Second, in his remarkable conception of an Utopian industrial city, fully elaborated and as fully expressed in architectural projects. In Ledoux we see Neo-classicism transcending its archaeological terms and becoming the architectural equivalent of the thought of a Rousseau or a Condorcet.

Of Ledoux's generation no other architect attempted such startling innovations. French architecture still held to its long tradition and the *atelier* of Jacques François Blondel, where many of them (including Ledoux) received their training, inculcated moderation. Nevertheless, from about 1775, the general trend towards geometrical starkness, combined with an archaeologically-minded but sometimes bizarre use of classical ornaments is unmistakable. Patronage in these years was of a highly sophisticated and exacting kind with a strong predilection for brilliant novelties. Much talent was lavished on houses and villas in and around Paris, few of which have survived. Bélanger's Bagatelle, in the Bois de Boulogne, is a notable exception.

95 F. J. Bélanger's Bagatelle, the villa in the Bois de Boulogne, Paris, built for the Comte d'Artois, in 1777; from J. Ch. Krafft's *Recueil d'architecture civile*, 1812. The story is that Bélanger built it in sixty-four days to win a bet with Marie Antoinette. He was also an eminent designer of gardens.

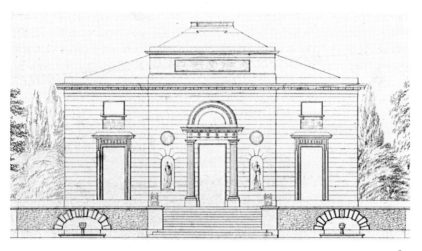

96 The Hôtel de Salm, Paris, designed by Pierre Rousseau for Prince Frederick Salm-Kyrberg in the early 1780s. On the river front, seen here, a severe façade with busts in niches is broken by an apsidal bay reflecting a circular salon inside. On the other side a six-column portico projects into a colonnaded court.

A sensational Paris building in its time was Jacques Gondoin's Ecole de Médecine of 1769–76, with its unmodulated Ionic colonnade towards the street, its immaculate portico and lecture-hall like a semi-Panthéon. Another was the Hôtel de Salm (now the Chancellery of the Legion of Honour) of 1782–86. Among public buildings before 1789 some of the most prominent were theatres. Indeed, Victor Louis' theatre at Bordeaux, built in 1777–80, with its horseshoe auditorium and magnificently ample lay-out of concert hall and reception areas is usually held to be the first great modern theatre (see p. 112).

Art, nature and the Gothic

Paris can fairly be said to have been the centre of Neo-classical developments in the last quarter of the century. England, however, having established a sturdy architectural independence in the years of Palladianism proceeded towards Neo-classical interpretations of her own. The most effective of these attitudes goes with the name of Robert Adam, the leading member of a family of Scottish architects who, after a period of four years in Italy, with Clérisseau as his tutor and Piranesi as a major influence, returned in 1758 to conquer

London. This was at a time when the fashion for building enormous Palladian country seats was just past its peak. Interest in bleak and massive exteriors was giving way to a desire for new standards of interior elegance and it was in the re-planning and decoration of existing houses that Adam made his name. Adam's planning was an elaboration of Burlington's but the 'Adam style' meant a light and harmonious combination of themes from antique wall and vault decoration and from some of the 16th-century Italian masters. It is seen at its idiosyncratic best in such princely mansions as Syon House, Middlesex, and Kedleston Hall, Derbyshire, but nowhere better than some of his adroitly planned town houses of which No. 20 Portman Square (now the Courtauld Institute of Art) is the finest.

Adam was almost entirely independent of French influences. His chief contemporary and rival, Sir William Chambers, on the other hand, had studied under J. F. Blondel and modified the Palladian tradition a little way towards the style of J. - A. Gabriel. His principal

97 The Ecole de Médicine, Paris, 1769–76, by Jacques Gondoin. The Ionic order of the street front is continued round the four sides of the great courtyard, threading its way through a Corinthian portico. Behind this is the lecture theatre, planned like an antique theatre, with a half-dome based on the Pantheon.

98, 99 Robert Adam brought a new inventive genius to the problem of interior decoration. Drawing on a wide repertory of classical motifs, he evolved a style that could be elegantly refined (as in the drawing room of No. 20 Portman Square, London, left) or endowed with a heavier Roman solemnity (as in the anteroom of Syon House, near London, below).

100 Right: Sir William Chambers' Somerset House, London, 1776–80, was built on the site of a royal palace to accommodate various departments of state and the learned societies. Its scale is domestic rather than monumental. In style it represents a union of Palladianism and the taste of J.-A. Gabriel.

work, Somerset House, London (a palace rebuilt to house government offices), is of considerable distinction but lacks the monumentality which English architecture had been able to achieve under Wren and his immediate successors. Indeed, neither Chambers nor Adam rank high as monumental architects and for this there is a significant reason. Political power had become vested in the landed nobility rather than the Crown, and the English nobility preferred the country to the town. It was on their country seats that their money was spent and their interest in metropolitan public works was negligible. Furthermore, after 1760 it was the 'villa' rather than the commanding mansion which attracted interest and alongside this interest was a passionate interest in landscape. The landscape-gardening fashions of the English 18th century were, in fact, probably more significant in the whole European scene than anything achieved in English architecture, with the possible exception of the English conception of Palladianism.

The English initiative in landscape-gardening was set off by the revolt of some of the literary figures of the early part of the century –

101 The movement away from formal garden design is illustrated by these two views of the same part of Stowe, Buckinghamshire, in 1739 and 1753. In the earlier one, straight paths lead away into the distance, left and right, and trees and hedges are arranged in neatly ordered patterns.

Temple, Addison, Pope – against the rigid formality of lay-out inherited from the French and the Dutch. The result was the landscape-garden of William Kent, as seen at Rousham, Oxfordshire, and Stowe, Buckinghamshire. The principle of treating a natural landscape *as* a natural landscape but changing its character to intensify the effect was soon widely accepted. Between 1750 and 1780 nearly all the great English parks passed through the hands of Lancelot ('Capability') Brown who swept away the avenues and *parterres* and remodelled the grounds according to a vision of his own. This vision crystallized in a formula which embraced the new planting of clumps and belts of trees combined with the creation of new contours and artificial serpentine lakes. After Brown's death in 1783, a new leader arose in the person of Humphry Repton, whose theory of landscape-gardening is associated with the philosophy of the 'Picturesque' as expounded by Richard Payne Knight and Uvedale Price. Their approach was subtler than Brown's, whom they critized for failure to

102 By 1753, although the rows of trees remain where they were, William Kent has softened the formality and the effect aimed at is one of sophisticated wildness. The little temple on the left, the so-called 'Rotonda', is by Vanbrugh, but altered. 'Capability' Brown worked at Stowe early in his career.

perceive the intrinsic character of each several landscape. To them this was the proper starting point, an 'improved' landscape being an original work of nature with blemishes and obstructions removed. It was from Brown and Repton that the phenomenon known as the *jardin anglais* spread throughout Europe. The Duke of Brunswick expressed an intention to lay out a park in the English taste as early as 1767. By the end of the century informal planting was a general practice.

Another factor which distinguishes the English scene from that of France and the Continent generally is the attitude towards Gothic. The French admired Gothic for its *hardiesse*, as a matter of structural accomplishment and were sometimes concerned, as was Soufflot at the Panthéon, to find equivalents in classical terms. When new stalls, pulpits or altars were required in ancient churches, they were in the prevailing classical fashion. This was not always so in England, where a tradition of sophisticated 'modern Gothic' descended from Sir

Christopher Wren. The west towers of Westminster Abbey, designed by Hawksmoor, were built in 1734–45; Kent designed a Gothic screen for Hereford Cathedral in 1742 and Gothic interiors for the Law Courts in Westminster Hall. This was a stylized Gothic with no pretensions to archaeological correctness. It was Horace Walpole who, in a long series of improvisations at his Thames-side house, Strawberry Hill, Twickenham (1748–77), introduced a Gothic revival based on historical sentiment and archaeological enquiry. Walpole's attitude was professionalized by James Wyatt, who, in the last quarter of the century, built quantities of Gothic country houses, 'abbeys' and 'castles', the most celebrated being the fabulous Fonthill Abbey, Wiltshire, for the millionaire romantic William Beckford. It was begun in 1800 – the harbinger of a century in which English attitudes to Gothic were to play a bizarre and conspicuous role.

Outside France and England, the history of Neo-classicism is almost everywhere dependent on what was happening in those two countries. In Russia, Catherine II was a patroness of architecture on a scale even more preposterous than that of her predecessor Elizabeth. The earlier buildings of her reign were either by French or Italian architects or by the two great Russians V. I. Bazhenov and I. Y. Starov, who had studied together in Paris and visited Italy. Later, in 1779, she took into her service Charles Cameron, a pupil of the minor English Palladian Isaac Ware; and about the same time the Italian Giacomo Quarenghi. The palaces and public buildings of these men were full-scale realizations of projects which in the West would have got no further than the paper sheets submitted in competition at the various academies. Bazhenov's Tauride Palace must, in its time, have been one of the noblest exemplifications of French Neo-classicism in Europe. Cameron's pavilion at Tsarskoe Selo – set, inevitably, in a park landscaped à l'anglaise – is an ambitious but technically feeble exercise in the Adam style. Quarenghi, in the English Palace at Peterhof, reverted to a severe Palladianism – less like Palladio, however, than like his British reviver, Colen Campbell.

What was true of Russia on a huge scale was true for Germany and even for Italy on a very small one. Everywhere there were Neo-classical stirrings but rarely the opportunities for their acceleration towards full expression. Everywhere, 'noble simplicity' was spoken

The revival of Gothic in England arose, first, because of the need to make additions to ancient buildings appropriate in style but, later, as deliberate exercises in Gothic forms to evoke the romance of history.

103 The west towers of Westminster Abbey, designed by Nicholas Hawksmoor and executed by John James between 1736 and 1745.

104 Fonthill Abbey (upper right), William Beckford's extravagant recreation of a visionary Middle Ages, designed by James Wyatt, 1796–1807 (from Britton's *Illustrations of Fonthill Abbey*, 1823).

105 Horace Walpole's Gallery at Strawberry Hill, Twickenham, one of the earliest and certainly the most influential of Gothic Revival houses, 1748–77.

106 The so-called 'Cameron Gallery' was added by Charles Cameron to the palace at Tsarskoe Selo about 1780, its rather precious classicism contrasting with the arrogant Baroque of Rastrelli's building (pl. 28).

of, everywhere parks in the English style were desired. But it was not till after 1800 that the full tide of Neo-classicism spent itself across the face of Europe. And by then the whole character of the movement had begun to change. Its inherent eclecticism had come to the surface. If we look around Europe of the 1790s we can see it at work, no less in the minimal structures of a rural economy than in sweeping projects of urban extension.

The cult of the cottage

In Britain the philosophy of the 'Picturesque', already mentioned as part of the landscape movement, reached a critical phase in 1794 with the publication of Payne Knight's didactic poem *The Landscape* and Uvedale Price's prose response, the *Essay on the Picturesque*. Both works treated mainly of landscape but also brought to the surface a latent curiosity about buildings *within* landscape; not only the great mansion and the gentleman's villa, but those lowlier products of the countryside, the dwellings of the labouring class. These were essential to the well-being of society and no less essential to the pictorial image of rurality. The minimal dwelling had always exercised a certain fascination. Serlio, in his unpublished sixth book of architecture, written in France before the middle of the 16th century and dealing exclusively with domestic buildings, had given a design for a two-roomed cottage which he called 'Maison du pauvre payson pour trois degrés de pauvreté'. With its pyramidal thatched roof and a four-post porch it is curiously prophetic of some of the inventions of the late 18th century. It might be possible to trace a continuous consciousness of cottage architecture through the two centuries which separate Serlio from the age of Enlightenment, but it is enough for our purpose to investigate its emergence, mainly in France and England, in the second half of the 18th century.

If the fashion for the irregular garden and the landscaped park started in England, it was almost at once adopted in France, where readers of Rousseau found in it a happy reflection of the philosopher's notion of the simple life. Parks planted or remodelled in the English style seemed to invite architectural features of equivalent simplicity

107 The 'hameau', an artificial farm near the Petit Trianon at Versailles, was the setting for Marie Antoinette's pretence of living the simple life and almost her only act of architectural patronage. Her architect was Richard Mique.

108 Estate villages like Milton Abbas, Dorset, 1774–80, had a practical purpose – to rehouse tenants evicted by the landowner (in this case to improve his view) in good, plain houses. Selfconscious rusticity came later.

and naturalness. Marie Antoinette's celebrated '*hameau*' at the Petit Trianon, Versailles, affects these qualities, though it cannot be said to owe anything to English, or for that matter to French, vernaculars.

The cult of the cottage has several aspects. One is the purely romantic or sentimental one: the cottage as a random affair, a patchwork of mixed materials, growing, as it were, out of the landscape. Second, there is the cottage as a rational design with something of the feeling of Laugier's 'primitive hut'. Third is the strictly functional cottage based on a study of the needs of the agricultural labourer and considered as an economic rather than an artistic enterprise. The second and third types can be and often were combined. Then again there are interesting social gradations. The cottage could be half-way to a villa, a place of restful retirement for a man of substance. The architect John Plaw, a great publisher of cottage designs, introduced the expressions '*ferme ornée*' and '*cottage orné*', hybrids which suggest a small house of decorative pretension and a decided manifestation of French taste.

The earliest architecturally conscious cottages in England are those forming village groups attendant upon large country houses. Of these, the best known is at Milton Abbas, Dorset (1774–80), where plain houses, three windows wide, with thatched roofs, are equally spaced on either side of a long hill. Chambers and Capability Brown seem both to have had a hand in this. At Harewood, Yorkshire, there is rather more attempt at architectural grouping by John Carr (*c*.1770) in the estate houses near the park gates.

But the cult of the cottage only acquired its true nature in England with a series of publications which started about 1790 and continued for about 30 years. The first was a hard-headed handbook for landowners interested in the functional and economic aspects of the subject, published by the younger John Wood in 1782; it went into three editions. More deeply rooted in the Picturesque philosophy was James Malton's *Essay on British Cottage Architecture*, 1795. The subtitle explains it as 'an attempt to perpetuate on Principle, that peculiar mode of Building which was originally the effect of Chance'. For Malton the typical cottage was a mixture of half-timbering, brick, weather boarding and thatch, brought together, no doubt, by a succession of alterations and enlargements. He maintained that these gems of accidental architecture were fast disappearing; their principles should be abstracted and used in the design of new cottages. In Malton we find the type of cottage which endeared itself to the suburban speculator of the Victorian age and remained a standard British product till the Second World War.

109 Plate from Malton's *Essay on British Cottage Architecture*, 1795, in which the author deplored the loss of old cottages and recommended that new ones should be designed as a *pastiche* of vernacular effects to preserve the character of the countryside.

110 The Brandenberg Gate, Berlin, 1789–93, by C. G. Langhans – Greek in inspiration but magnified to a Roman scale to accord with the political status of the Prussian capital. The quadriga, in copper, was the work of Schadow. The lateral colonnades were added in 1868.

Archaeology, abstraction and the exotic

Around 1800 there are three different characters in which Neoclassicism presents itself. First, there is the archaeological purism, which is the mainspring of the Napoleonic transformation of Paris and which produced dramatic classical gestures such as the Brandenburg Gate at Berlin. Then, second, there is the quest of abstraction, dramatically exhibited in Ledoux's great work but more explicitly in some of the executed works of John Soane, whose first Bank of England halls belong to 1791, and most poignantly in the designs of Friedrich Gilly of Berlin who died in 1800 at the age of twenty-eight. Thirdly, there is the Neo-classicism which is not classical at all but which affects to be Gothic, Egyptian, Chinese, Turkish or Indian. If it seems absurd to apply the term Neo-classical to such extraneous products it would be even more absurd to pretend that they form an autonomous development. In all cases, wherever they are found, they are the work of Neo-classical masters, often, indeed, of the leading masters. It was Sir William Chambers, most prudent and academic of Neo-classicists, who designed the pagoda at Kew Gardens. At the

111 The Pagoda in Kew Gardens, by Sir William Chambers, 1757–63, is one of the survivors from a whole gallery of exotic buildings including an 'Alhambra', a 'Mosque' and a 'Gothic cathedral' which Chambers designed for the Dowager Princess of Wales at Kew.

other end of Europe it was Quarenghi who designed the 'Great Caprice' (a Roman arch surmounted by a Chinese tempietto) at Tsarskoe Selo. Most of these things we now regard as 'follies', but with questionable justice. Irrational experiments, undertaken for entertainment rather than use, they mostly were; but they were, equally, factors of disorientation, evidences of that sense of the plurality of styles which eventually created the problem of 'style' which was to haunt the whole of the 19th century.

Of the three characters presented by 18th-century Neo-classicism, the archaeological is the most persistent, the most fundamental and, paradoxically, the one felt to be most rational. When Thomas Jefferson, after the American War of Independence, came to Europe and considered, in the course of his travels, the proper basis for the architecture of a new republic he found it, not in the contemporary architecture of England, but in that perfect exemplification of a Roman temple which was also Laugier's symbol of perfect rationality – the Maison Carrée at Nîmes. Accordingly, when in 1785 designs were required for the State Capitol of Virginia at Richmond,

112 The State House, Beacon Hill, Boston, 1793–1800, by Charles Bulfinch. American architects of the 18th century necessarily relied on European precedent, and the inspiration here seems to be Chambers' Somerset House.

Jefferson dictated a pro-style Ionic temple, divided into floors and with windows in its walls. It may not have been the most practical solution but it was the one nearest to the natural source of all architectural excellence. 'Noble simplicity' had crossed the seas.

Jefferson was a great amateur. Another, with a rather less severe concern with architectural principle, was Charles Bulfinch, a Harvard graduate who, having toured Europe (where he met Jefferson), interested himself in the architectural development of his native city, Boston, where he designed the State House on Beacon Hill in 1793–1800. It reflects London's Somerset House and all Bulfinch's work derives from contemporary English sources. The professional architect in the European sense had not yet made his appearance in America. He did so only in the last years of the century, notably in the person of Benjamin Henry Latrobe, whom Jefferson, as President, appointed to the newly created office of 'Surveyor of the Public

Buildings'. Latrobe came from Yorkshire but had Pennsylvanian antecedents. He acquired first-rate technical experience under S. P. Cockerell in London and under Smeaton in the Fens and might have done extremely well in England. But a bereavement followed by bankruptcy drove him to America. His style is a warm and imaginative Neo-classic, not unlike the early Soane, but apart from the Bank of Pennsylvania, built in 1798–99, his career belongs mostly to the 19th century. But not entirely. He arrived in America at a crucial moment in the building of the central monument of the new capital, Washington – the Capitol itself. This, in 1798, was already partly built. Three architects in succession had been in charge and the principle of a great rotunda with wings was now irreversible. The third of the three architects, George Hadfield, declined to accept his predecessors' work and was dismissed. Latrobe took over and his completion of the Capitol (not, however, in its present form) was the greatest work of his career. The Washington story however is one to which we shall return in due course.

113 The Bank of Pennsylvania, Philadelphia, 1798–99, by Benjamin Latrobe. Latrobe, an English immigrant, evolved an austere geometrical classicism not unlike that of Soane. The bank is one of his earliest works.

CHAPTER FIVE

Architecture and Society: the Enlightenment

At the beginning of this book a rough generalization was proposed, pinning a 'Baroque' label to the first half of the century and a 'Neo-classical' label to the second. Another generalization was set alongside this: churches and palaces, it was said, were the main architectural exhibits of the first half and public and institutional buildings of the second. So far we have been following the theme of our first generalization – i.e. *style*. The claims of the second theme – i.e. *typology* – must now be pressed. We must enquire what new types of building were initiated or what old types came into special promi-nence in the course of the century.

The creation of types is a social matter. It is also a matter of cultural climate. The 18th century was the century of the 'Enlightenment', a familiar expression which is by no means self-explanatory and which, if we attempt to analyse it, becomes infinitely complicated. We may take refuge in the great names – Newton and Locke, Voltaire, Montesquieu, Hume, Rousseau, Diderot – but if we are considering architecture we shall find no obvious way of connecting their thought with what was going on in the building world. 'Enlightenment' was not an all-pervading flood-light. It was a question of the formation of new attitudes by the acceptance of ideas filtering down from the philosophers to levels where they engaged with the practical business of living. It could, for instance, enter the mind of any actively intelligent person that if Newton, by the exercise of thought in higher reaches of intellect, had solved for all time (as it seemed) the problem of the Cosmos, the same agency of mind, scaled down to ordinary abilities and everyday problems, could solve these with equal confidence and certainty. In other words, society could be visualized

114 The court theatre at Bayreuth, 1742–48, by Giuseppe and Carlo Galli Bibiena. Here is the typical form of the mid 18th-century theatre, a U-shape of boxes facing a stage with a picture-frame proscenium arch. The ornately decorated margrave's box is placed to give the optimum view of the perspective scenery.

105

in an *enlightened* perspective in which technology, the arts, the law and its penalties, and the arts of administration began to be freshly seen, with a new humanitarianism and (to use a word of the period) *bienfaisance*, a kind of benevolent common-sense at a period in which common-sense was not all that common.

The culmination of Enlightenment came at the mid-century – in architecture as in the literary arts. The first volumes of Diderot's *Encyclopédie*, the *summa* of 'Enlightened' opinion, were published in 1751–52; Laugier's *Essai* appeared in 1753 and Soufflot started to build Ste Geneviève (the Panthéon) in 1757. Thereafter we begin to discern 'Enlightened' attitudes among the major architects. Some types of building were more susceptible to change than others and for our present purpose the following types have been selected: theatres, libraries, museums, hospitals, prisons and commercial buildings.

Theatres, public and private

At the start of the century the Baroque theatre was a fully developed type in Italy and already being imitated in northern cities. It is necessary however to distinguish two sub-types: the private Court theatre and the public theatre. Both had, in general, the same plan-shapes but differed in scale and character. The Court theatre was smaller and usually formed a part of a palace complex, so that no exterior display was called for. The public theatre occupied a conspicuous urban site and was often, externally, an architectural show-piece. The private theatre, built at the cost of the ruling dynasty, aimed at ease and elegance. The public theatre aimed at spectacle and, more to the point, maximum seating capacity, since the financing of the public theatres usually depended on the letting of private boxes. In many cases, three sides of the auditorium were completely lined with boxes, in anything up to six tiers.

The Court theatre of the mid-century included some of the most refined and artistic products of late Baroque and Rococo. The famous Rococo interiors at Bayreuth (1742–48), by the Italian Giuseppe and Carlo Galli Bibiena, and the rather similar Residenztheater at Munich (1750–52), by François Cuvilliés, are the best known. The undulating horizontals, wreathed columns and beautifully carved Atlantid figures made the latter a high point of Rococo achievement.

115 The Residenztheater, Munich, 1750–52, is one of the masterpieces of François Cuvilliés, whose work has already been illustrated (pls. 24, 25). Plan and construction here are conventional, the artistry lying in the Rococo decoration which was saved when the building was destroyed by bombing.

Destroyed in the Second World War, it was carefully rebuilt. Other such domestic theatres of the Courtly kind are still to be seen at Potsdam, at Schwetzingen, at Rheinsberg, at Charlottenburg and at Wilhelmsbad in Germany; Cesky Krumlov in Czechoslovakia; and Drottningholm (near Stockholm) in Sweden. All are of modest size and nearly all have flat ceilings decorated with illusionist perspective paintings. In Italy, the theatre at Caserta, near Naples (1752), is on a more imposing scale, while the theatre at Versailles (1763–70) is an altogether special case. Designed by J.-A. Gabriel, it has a powerful Ionic colonnade extending round the upper gallery and joined to the flat ceiling by a cove. At Gripsholm in Sweden (1782), Neo-classicism breaks through with a vengeance and we have a coffered semi-dome covering the small auditorium, which has 'amphitheatre' seating in the Greek manner.

116, 117, 118 Three court theatres of the second half of the century, when Neo-classical taste had succeeded the Baroque. Above left: Drottningholm, Sweden, 1764–66, by C. F. Adelcrantz, which had no galleries but only an open parterre to accommodate an audience. Below left: Gripsholm, Sweden, 1782, by Erik Palmstedt. The shape is determined by the round tower inside which it is built. Above: the Opéra at Versailles, 1763–70, by J.-A. Gabriel, where rows of boxes are combined with a so-called 'amphitheatre' of free-standing Ionic columns.

In the second half of the century it was the public theatre which rose to its highest peak of architectural ambition and 'Enlightened' form. In Italy, for instance, the Teatro Ducale at Milan was rebuilt with five tiers of boxes in 1714–17 and rebuilt again in 1776 as La Scala, with six tiers, by the architect Giuseppe Piermarini. At that date it was the largest theatre in the world, accommodating 4,000 (or 7,000 when arranged for balls). La Scala still stands, though Piermarini's decorations have been altered. The exterior is a severe piece of Neo-Palladianism. Almost in the same class but earlier in date is the theatre at Bologna, designed by Antonio Bibiena, another of the great family of scenographers, in 1756, with four tiers of boxes arranged within a series of superimposed arcades, rather like an inside-out version of the Roman Colosseum.

In France, the public theatre had become, by 1750, a widely popular institution reflecting the increased sense of social awareness and absorbing much of the loyalty formerly attached exclusively to the church. It was the theatre of Marivaux, Beaumarchais and the *comédie larmoyante*. Soufflot, the architect of the Panthéon, built a theatre at Lyons, begun in 1754, the first to stand on an island site and planned with ample foyer and public rooms. It was burnt down in 1828. In 1772 was begun one of the greatest of French theatres, the Grand Théâtre at Bordeaux, a municipal enterprise of impressive extravagance conducted by the architect, Victor Louis. Like Soufflot at Lyons, Louis had an island site at his disposal. A colonnade of twelve columns spreads itself across the main front and arcades penetrate the sides and rear. The auditorium is a truncated circle with a Corinthian order ascending through three tiers of boxes so that it gives the impression of a vast circular temple. But the auditorium occupies a relatively small part of the building, which contains an oval concert-hall, many public rooms and one of the grandest staircases in France, leading to the box of the Provincial Governor.

Only two years after the opening of the Bordeaux theatre, the new Comédie Française (the Odéon from 1797) opened in Paris. The theatre was financed by the Municipality of Paris with help from two departments of the Royal Household. The architects were Peyre and de Wailly, whose style had moved several shades further into Neo-classicism than Victor Louis'. Again there was a majestic colonnade

119 Auditorium of La Scala, Milan, by Giuseppe Piermarini, built 1776–78 on an unprecedentedly grand scale. The loss of intimacy in such surroundings brought a new acting and singing style that aroused comment at the time.

(this time Doric), with arcades through sides and back. The auditorium was a nearer approximation to the 'circular temple' idea than is the Bordeaux theatre – even to the extent that two detached columns appeared in the proscenium opening itself (they were removable however). And there were signs that concessions were being made to a new theatre-going bourgeoisie: the box fronts were continuous and the boxes were given removable partitions so that galleries could without difficulty be created.

These two theatres represent the high-water mark of theatre design in France and indeed in Europe. In principle it could be said that there was no significant departure from them for over a century.

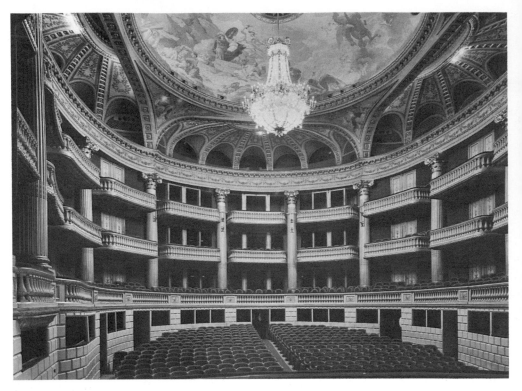

120, 121, 122 The Grand Théâtre, Bordeaux, begun 1772, by Victor Louis, a major public building on an island site which set the style for theatre buildings through the next century. Above: The auditorium, punctuated by giant columns and covered by a shallow dome. Left: The main façade. Right: The monumental staircase.

INTÉRIEUR DE LA NOUVELLE SALLE DE COMÉD

123 Longitudinal section through Peyre and de Wailly's 1770 project for the Comédie Française, later known as the Odéon, Paris. The pattern of theatre design was to remain virtually unchanged until the middle of the 20th century. On the right, a spacious foyer leads to two grand staircases giving access to the circles and boxes

ANÇAISE DE L'ANCIEN PROJET.

with, above the foyer, a salon open at two levels. The circular auditorium (modified to a more conventional U-shape when built) contained several tiers of boxes and a larger 'amphitheatre' at the top. An extensive stage area (off the picture on the left) accommodated the scenery and machinery.

In England, the building of theatres advanced on less favourable ground, though the age of Garrick and Sheridan supplied abundant popular enthusiasm. Theatres claimed royal patronage and were licensed under patent but this did not mean that the Crown supplied finance; the London theatres were all speculative ventures by syndicates of shareholders. The municipal theatre was unknown. Drury Lane, originally designed by Wren, was remodelled under Garrick by Robert Adam in 1775–76 with a fan-shaped auditorium, three tiers of boxes at the sides, two galleries at the back and a flat ceiling decorated to look like a coffered dome. On the continent it could have passed for an elegant but unambitious court theatre. When rebuilt and enlarged by Henry Holland for Sheridan in 1792, it conformed more nearly to continental standards, with five tiers of boxes, a raking pit and four galleries at the back. Perhaps the most interesting – and most English – thing about it was that boxes and galleries had their fronts supported on the slimmest of *iron* columns, in the form of antique candelabra.

The first London theatre to get anywhere near Paris standards was the King's Theatre in the Haymarket as rebuilt in 1790 by the Polish architect Michael Novosielski, who introduced the horseshoe planned auditorium into England. The theatre was demolished in 1894 to give place to the present Her Majesty's Theatre.

Libraries and museums

Libraries, as one would expect, played a conspicuous part in the age of Enlightenment. Nevertheless, the library as a detached single-purpose building remained rare till the 19th century. It happens that the famous library at the court of Duke Anton Ulrich of Brunswick at Wolfenbüttel, built as early as 1706–10 under the supervision of no less a philosopher than Leibniz, was a detached building. Pevsner calls it 'the first totally detached secular library ever'. It consisted of an oval book-lined reading room, rising within a rectangular structure to a ring of windows under a domical roof. It was demolished in 1887.

The next great library of the century is the Habsburg Court library, the Hofbibliothek at Vienna, designed by Fischer von Erlach and built in 1722–26. It has in common with Wolfenbüttel an oval central space but the oval is placed *across* the rectangle so that the plan somewhat

124, 125 Drury Lane Theatre, London. Right: The early theatre as redesigned by Robert Adam, 1775–76 (the figures in this plate from R. and J. Adam's *Works in Architecture*, 1788, are made artificially small to exaggerate the size of the theatre). Below: As rebuilt by Henry Holland in 1792, a much bigger building, with the tiers supported on iron columns.

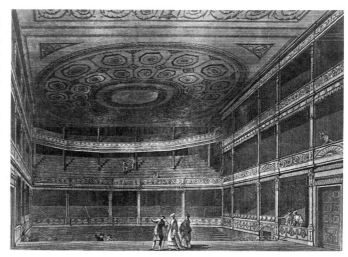

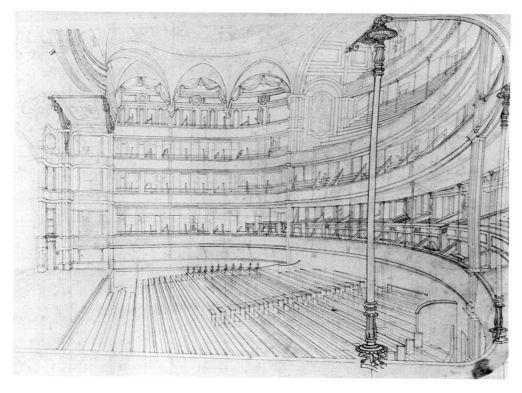

resembles the great abbatial churches of the period, with a 'nave' on either side of an oval 'transept'. The book-cases are placed against the walls throughout, at two levels, with cantilevered galleries for access to the upper level.

The Vienna Court library is followed by the long series of Baroque and Rococo libraries built by those rich German and Austrian abbeys to whose churches we have already given some attention. These libraries are orientated towards Counter-Reformation ideals rather than those of the Enlightenment. They belong to a tradition, begun in the 17th century, of a library as a long hall with book-lined walls, this type replacing the medieval system of book-shelves projecting from the walls to form 'stalls' for study. The books are accessible at two levels, the upper level from a gallery which is supported on ornate cantilevers, as at Melk (c.1730) or by columns arranged for display, as at Ottobeuren (1721–24). Invariably the ceilings have ornate plaster-work enclosing painted panels. A later example is at Amorbach, where the ornament is as rich as ever, but expressed in the style of Louis XVI.

Three Baroque libraries, where architectural display is at least as important as the provision of books.

126 Left: The abbey of Ottobeuren, in Bavaria, 1721–24, by Johann Michael Fischer.

127 Right: The Court Library of Vienna, 1722–26, by J. B. Fischer von Erlach, a complex space divided by arches and giant columns.

128 Below: The library of Melk, in Austria, about 1730, by Jakob Prandtauer. It occupies the left-hand wing projecting towards the river in pl. 45.

129, 130 Two libraries of the 'English Baroque' school: Hawksmoor's Codrington Library at All Souls, Oxford, begun 1715 (top), and Gibbs' Radcliffe Camera, also at Oxford, begun 1737. The Codrington is a simple container of books; the Radcliffe is more a monument to the benefactor.

131 Exterior of the Radcliffe Camera. The idea of a free-standing circular library was introduced by Wren in his unbuilt scheme for the Library of Trinity College, Cambridge; it was taken over by Hawksmoor, whom Gibbs followed at the Radcliffe Camera.

Abbey libraries of this type were built not only in Austria but in Germany, Switzerland and Portugal. Indeed the libraries at Coimbra and Mafra, Portugal, built in 1716–17 are among the earliest. In Protestant England, the nearest approximation is the Codrington library at All Souls' College, Oxford, begun in 1715: a hall 200 feet long with one side nearly all windows and the other nearly all books; no paintings or architectural sculpture whatever: a very 'Protestant' version.

Then, again at Oxford, comes one of the most remarkable library buildings of the century – the Radcliffe Camera. This was built from a bequest by a successful physician, Dr John Radcliffe. Conceived first by Hawksmoor as a domed rotunda, then by Gibbs as a long gallery with stalls, on the lines of Wren's library at Cambridge, the rotunda model was finally adopted, but re-designed by Gibbs after Hawksmoor's death. As a library it is extravagant, the space for books being limited to alcoves round an open central space. It was no doubt envisaged as a sort of cenotaph for Radcliffe, who endowed the University not only with this building but also with an infirmary and an observatory. He was a figure characteristic of the Enlightenment. Gibbs hardly was.

In the latter part of the 18th century there were many proposals for royal or university libraries but none of any great consequence was realized.

A building type which has a special association with the Enlightenment is the public museum. The museum idea goes back to the Renaissance and gathers momentum in the 16th and 17th centuries, when the great Roman families hoarded antique marbles and displayed them either in their palaces or in their courtyards or gardens. The purpose of such collections, however, was far from that of a museum as we understand the word; it was rather to satisfy the owner's pride of possession and his craving to participate in the golden age of antiquity. Such collections were not open to the public, though scholars of presentable appearance, carrying introductions, could usually gain admittance. Paintings were also collected in the 17th century and hung in long galleries provided for the purpose.

By the beginning of the 18th century, collecting of this kind had spread among the German princelings and there are galleries of art in a score of regional palaces, starting with Salzdahlum (1688–94) and going on through Frederick the Great's Sans-Souci of 1756–64 to nearly the end of the century. In England much the same thing was happening, with rich collections of statues, sarcophagi, cinerary urns and vases in specially designed galleries at such houses as Holkham (1734) and Newby, Yorkshire (1767–85, an addition by Robert Adam). Freedom of access was restricted but most English owners displayed the same liberality in the matter as their continental counterparts.

Apart from galleries of painting and sculpture there was the type of museum known in Germany as the *Wunderkammer* or *Schatzkammer*. This had little or nothing to do with art. The sort of things it sheltered were natural curiosities, varieties and freaks, mechanical toys, coins and medals, ancient armour and fire-arms. But it was the *Wunderkammer* as much as the gallery of art which eventually established the precise nature of the museum.

The first *public* display of antiquities was the Capitoline Museum in Rome, associated with the Accademia Capitolina, a training school for artists, and founded in 1734. Ten years later, Count Scipione Maffei, inspired no doubt by the Capitoline, began to form his collection of sculpture in Verona in a square cloister with Doric colonnades. This was open to the public from the start.

Parallel with Maffei's enterprise but altogether more imposing and essentially private is the villa which Cardinal Albani built near Rome and which was completed in 1769. Designed by a little-known architect, Carlo Marchionni, the villa is Baroque in detail but composed in a more or less Neo-classical spirit. Its main front is a regular sequence of nine bays, with a loggia on the ground floor and a long gallery above with suites of rooms on both floors behind. It is more a museum than a residence; the Cardinal and his court would spend a day there, returning to Rome in the evening. In 1758, Albani had appointed Johann Joachim Winckelmann as his librarian and keeper of antiquities. The latter's famous essay on the imitation of Greek work in painting and sculpture had appeared three years earlier and he was soon to become the leader of Enlightenment in antiquarian scholarship in Europe. With Winckelmann in charge, the Villa Albani became the most sophisticated museum in Europe. Carlo Cavaceppi

was employed on the restoration of antique statues and the pieces were grouped in typological series. Some of them were built into Marchionni's decorative interior architecture. Conspicuously placed in one of the rooms was Mengs' *Apollo and the Muses*, a seminal work in Neo-classical painting.

By 1760 the idea of a great *public* and *national* museum of arts and antiquities had become one of the ideals of the Enlightenment and the ideal had in fact been realized – but not yet in architectural form. The British Museum had come into existence when in 1753 the British parliament passed an act authorizing the purchase (by means of a public lottery) of Sir Hans Sloane's collection of natural objects and the construction or acquisition of a suitable building in which to house it, together with the Cotton and Harleian collections, already in the government's hands. The whole collection was to be freely accessible 'to all studious and curious Persons'. An abandoned ducal residence, Montagu House in Bloomsbury, was purchased for its reception and the British Museum opened its doors for the first time in 1759.

The British Museum had to wait another sixty years for a home of its own but the institution of a free, national treasure-house of arts and sciences represented a spectacular advance. It was perhaps this model which inspired the Landgrave Frederic II of Hesse to build the museum at Kassel which bears his name. This was a departure from the

132 Left: The Villa Albani, Rome, the first purpose-built museum. It was completed in 1769 by Carlo Marchionni for the display of Cardinal Albani's collection of sculpture. The view here is by Piranesi.

133 Right: The Museum Fredericanum at Kassel, founded by the Landgrave, Frederick II, and begun in 1769. It contained a library, a collection of antiquities and a display of objects of scientific interest. Designed by Simon Louis du Ry, a Frenchman, it was freely open to the public from the start.

princely tradition of installing galleries in private palaces. The Museum Fredericanum is an independent building of severe classical discipline, dedicated from the first to public enjoyment. It was, to be sure, under the direct control of the Landgrave, who had his own study in the building, and therefore hardly 'national', but it was organized as a public institution and looks like one. The entrance front, with its grand portico (the first of its kind in the history of museums), has somewhat the air of the Munich Glyptothek of forty-four years later.

The ground floor at Kassel is a gallery originally devoted to antique statuary. Above this was the library. Elsewhere were rooms devoted to natural science (minerals, maritime plants, butterflies, etc.) and curiosities (coins, clocks, etc.); musical instruments and wax-works were also displayed, so there was an element of the *Wunderkammer*. Here was the image of what, in visual terms, the national museum of the future might be.

An image of a different, but not wholly unrelated, kind now made its appearance in Rome. This was the Museo Pio-Clementino in the Vatican, founded by Clement XIV and completed by Pius VI for the reception of the papacy's vast holding of antique marbles, much of it still exhibited out-of-doors. The museum consists of a series of halls, partly on the north–south axis of Bramante's octagonal Belvedere

125

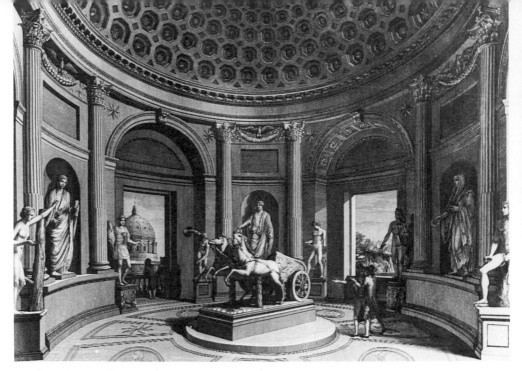

134 The Museo Pio-Clementino was added to the Vatican palace between 1773 and 1780 by the architects Simonetti and Camporesi to contain the unparalleled papal collection of antiquities. Its style follows Roman models to provide a setting appropriate to the objects.

Court and partly on an east–west axis, the two axes meeting in a domed rotunda. The whole suite was in the spirit of the ancient *thermae* (baths), the shape of each hall being a distinct antique type. The architects of this purest piece of Neo-classicism were Michelangelo Simonetti and Giuseppe Camporesi and it was finished in 1780. The halls were not open to the general public but a letter of introduction usually secured admission. The Museo Pio-Clementino immediately became the most admired museum building in Europe but it proved not large enough for the Vatican's needs and in 1806–23 a new gallery, designed by Raffaello Stern was built across the Cortile del Belvedere.

By the end of the century, the 'National Museum' idea was being assiduously cultivated by the Academies. The subject set for the Prix de Rome in the first year of its award, 1778–79, was a museum. The programme prescribed three departments: the Sciences, the Liberal

Arts and Natural History, with a print room, cabinet of medals, provision for the conservation of natural objects and a residence for the director. This is very much on the lines of the British Museum. It is significant, however, that classical antiquities are not awarded their traditional priority: the museum was claiming a specifically modern function.

Boullée, in 1783, produced an extravagant design based on the same ideas but, characteristically, assembling them round a central space dedicated solely to statues of great men. With the Revolution the idea of a public national museum for the people was confirmed, at least in France, where the Louvre became the national palace of art, which it still is.

Hospitals and prisons

A golden thread in the history of the Enlightenment is *'bienfaisance'*, meaning quite simply the desire to render society more reasonable and more humane, and in no area of building had that spirit more scope than in the planning of hospitals and prisons. Both these types of institution are for people deprived, whether by disability or force of law, of their freedom. The plans for such buildings are likely to have much in common. Both may admit a greater or lesser degree of humanitarianism.

Take hospitals first. Their story is necessarily rather complicated because the 18th century inherited a variety of meanings for the word. A 'hospital' might mean an almshouse, a school, a place for the healing of the sick or a home for the incurable, an asylum for lunatics or a place of reception for illegitimate children. It could be any of these, but usually the 18th-century hospital was a place for the general reception of the sick poor. The rich had their servants and could command the attendance of physicians. The poor had no such facilities and their dependence on charity was total. Hence the great institutions called 'Albergi dei Poveri' in Italy and the equivalent 'Hôtels Dieu' in France. Descended from medieval institutions, they were often rebuilt by benefactors on palatial lines. Examples in Italy are the Pammatone in Genoa of 1750 and the Albergo dei Poveri in Naples of 1751, the latter designed by Fuga on the same vast scale as the neighbouring palace of Caserta. In Austria there is the Hospital of St John at Salzburg by Fischer von Erlach. These are all Baroque buildings in whose lay-out the church occupies the central place. Soufflot's Hôtel Dieu at Lyons is another of this kind; its grand river-side front is more monumental than London's Somerset House (whose inspiration it probably was). But by far the most celebrated of these public hospitals was the Hôtel Dieu at Paris, celebrated not only for its size but also for the appalling conditions which prevailed there. This festering, over-grown inheritance from the Middle Ages came to be the place at which the history of modern hospitals started.

Founded originally in the 9th century, the Hôtel Dieu had grown into a huge establishment to which all sick and dying paupers in Paris were assigned. Situated near Notre Dame, it occupied houses on a bridge across the Seine and although it had expanded on to the south bank it was still not large enough to supply the needs of the capital. Conditions were horrific: four to six patients in one bed, irrespective of their ailments, the death rate one in four. Then, in 1772, there was a conflagration and a great part of the Hôtel Dieu was destroyed. The public conscience was aroused and the problem of the future of Paris hospitals came under the scrutiny of administrators and architects. Controversy followed for the next sixteen years, and its course is a significant part of Enlightenment history.

First of all, the government asked the Académie des Sciences for advice and a plan was worked out by a scientist, Jean Baptiste Le Roy, in collaboration with an architect, Charles-François Viel, for a completely new hospital situated outside Paris. The plan was remarkable for its modernity. Parallel rows of single-storey wards were ranged on either side of a courtyard at the far end of which was a church. Special attention was paid to ventilation. No action was taken on this plan, however, and in 1774 another project was published, this time by a surgeon, Antoine Petit. He proposed a vast circular building to be sited outside Paris at Belleville. There was to be a domed building in the centre with six long four-storey wards radiating from it. This was also put aside.

In 1774 Louis XVI set up a commission to examine the whole subject of Paris hospitals. The commission did not favour grand schemes but suggested that small hospitals in various parishes were to be preferred. In 1773, Madame Necker, wife of the finance minister,

135, 136 Two of the public hospitals built for the poor by private charity. Left: the river wing of the Hôtel Dieu at Lyons, begun in 1741, by J. G. Soufflot, the architect of the Panthéon (pls. 62–64). Below: the Albergo dei Poveri at Naples, begun ten years later to designs by Ferdinando Fuga; its vast façade is even longer than that of the nearby palace of Caserta (pl. 31).

had endowed a small model hospital in Paris. In 1780 the curé of the parish of St Jacques-du-haut-pas (the Abbé Cochin) built a hospice to a design by C.-F. Viel, who gave his services for nothing. It was a remarkable design, though less for its plan than for the Greek Doric portal which adorned the street front, seeming to signify a radical puritanism in the approach to a subject with no stylistic precedents. The Hospice Beaujon, designed by J.-D. Antoine followed in 1784. Then came, in 1785, an anonymous *Mémoire* accompanying a circular plan on the lines of Petit's but with sixteen instead of six radial wards and accommodation for 5,000 beds, to be built on the Isle des Cygnes. The authors of this plan were Claude Philippe Coquéau and Bernard Poyet, the latter being Contrôleur des Bâtiments to the City of Paris. The King forwarded this plan to the Académie des Sciences. The committee which reported on it turned it down, however, and expressed themselves in favour of Le Roy's scheme of 1777. A second report included a revised scheme by Poyet on the Le Roy model. Finally, in 1788 came the classic *Mémoires* of J. R. Tenon, a surgeon-member of the Académie des Sciences. Tenon, with Poyet's assistance, produced a scheme for a hospital on the Poyet principle to be built in the Paris suburb of La Roquette. It was begun but never completed, but the plan was reproduced by Durand in his *Recueil et Parallèle* and formed the basis of most of the great Paris hospitals of the next century.

An interesting feature of Tenon's *Mémoires* is his reference to hospital buildings in England, which he visited in the course of his investigations and where he found arrangements superior to those in France. The two hospitals for lunatics, for instance – Bedlam and St Luke's – he pronounced the best within his knowledge. The hospital which interested him most, however, was the Naval Hospital at Stonehouse, whose plan consisted of parallel ward-blocks, linked by colonnades running round three sides of a great court. This had much in common with his own conception of a newly conceived Hôtel Dieu.

But Tenon must also have been struck (though he does not say so) by the way in which so many English hospitals came into being. Some of them, like St Bartholomew's and St Thomas's, were ancient foundations expanded or rebuilt by wealthy philanthropists or by

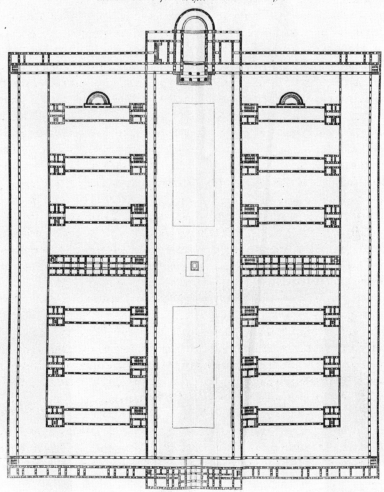

commencé à la Roquette en 1788, sur les dessins de Poyet.

137 Bernard Poyet's plan, published in 1787 (here reproduced from Durand's *Recueil*) for a hospital at La Roquette, near Paris; an attempt to solve the problems of infection and overcrowding by rational planning. The building was never completed, but it influenced later French hospitals well into the 19th century.

A large number of hospitals was built in England during the 18th century. Some were rebuildings of medieval foundations, others (for the armed forces) were built by the state; others, again, by small committees of private benefactors.

138–140 The naval hospitals of Gosport (top left) and Stonehouse, near Plymouth (centre left), both date from the middle years of the century and were planned on a large scale. That of Stonehouse uses the principle of isolated pavilions to reduce the risk of infection (two in the foreground are omitted for the sake of clarity); the central building is the chapel. The Middlesex Hospital (bottom left), designed by James Paine in 1752, was an exceptionally stylish London hospital.

141, 142 The Foundling Hospital (top) owed its origin to Thomas Coram whose promotion of the scheme lasted through seventeen years; it was opened in 1742. The London Hospital (above) was founded by a group of seven citizens who sent out 2,000 letters of appeal; it was built after 1748. The architect of the London Hospital was Boulton Mainwaring; of the Foundling, Theodore Jacobsen. Both gave their services free.

public subscription. Only the naval and military hospitals at Green-wich, Chelsea, Gosport and Stonehouse were financed by the state and from 1720 the English had developed the tradition of the voluntary hospital.

The first voluntary hospital in England was the Westminster. It originated at a meeting in a London coffee-house in 1719 of a merchant-banker, a brewer, a writer of religious tracts and an unorthodox clergyman. Its development need not concern us here because it occupied converted houses until a great Gothic building opposite Westminster Abbey was built for it in 1833 (demolished in 1950). Similarly, the London Hospital was started by seven men meeting at a tavern in 1740 and then sending out 2,000 letters appealing for support. The hospital opened in a small way in the same year but in 1748 was able to commission the architect Boulton Mainwaring to build the grimly plain but not inelegant brick mass which still forms the main part of the hospital. The Foundling Hospital was the creation of one man, Captain Thomas Coram, who exerted himself over seventeen years to stir public opinion and obtain a charter and the necessary finance. The architect, Theodore Jacobsen, was an amateur who gave his services free (as also did the professional surveyor). The hospital opened in 1742 and was soon famous for its music and for the works of art contributed by artists of the time. Both the London and the Foundling were plain, sturdy buildings clearly exercising a strict economy of means. The Middlesex, however, another example of inspiration by a small group of benevolent citizens, built itself in 1752 a home of some architectural distinction, indistinguishable externally from the town residence of a noble family, a type to which the architect, James Paine, was more accustomed.

It was in the provinces, however, that the voluntary-hospital movement scored its most remarkable successes. Between 1730 and the end of the century nearly every city and county town had equipped itself with a hospital building of substantial size. Some were benefactions by rich men (Radcliffe at Oxford, Addenbrooke at Cambridge) but mostly they were promoted by small groups of local gentry, forming committees and raising funds. It cannot be said that any distinct architectural type emerged. Plain brick façades with a central pediment were the usual thing, compositional ideas being very

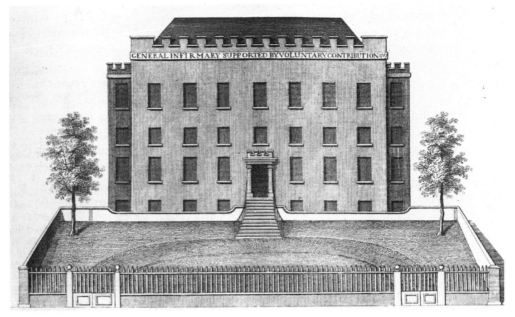

143 The Salisbury Infirmary of 1767, by John Wood the Younger, was one of many provincial hospitals built around the middle of the century with funds raised by small committees of citizens.

much those applicable to large country houses. An exception is the younger John Wood's Infirmary at Salisbury of 1767, a square mass with a central light-well, a crenellated parapet and windows all of equal size and, for ornament, an inscription in Roman capitals: GENERAL INFIRMARY SUPPORTED BY VOLUNTARY CONTRIBUTIONS 1767. Notwithstanding the advent of the Welfare State, the inscription survives: a reminder of one of the more impressive endeavours of the British Enlightenment of the 18th century.

The squalor, ignorance and neglect found in the typical hospital of the early 18th century was exceeded only by the cruelty and filth of prison life. The concept of a prison as an orderly institution to impose restraint and discipline on wrong-doers was scarcely recognized and the condemned man or woman was locked up in whatever building provided the necessary security at minimum expense – ancient castles, gate-houses and obsolete structures of all kinds were turned over to the purpose. Prisoners were still often chained. No account was taken of the prisoner's health and prisons without adequate light, ventilation or water-supply were commonplace.

Conditions in England are vividly described in the three books of the greatest of prison reformers, John Howard, the first of which, *The State of the Prisons*, came out in 1777. Howard was a Bedfordshire squire, born in 1726, who had found himself a prisoner of war in Portugal in 1756 and who, on his release, became obsessed with the need to expose the evils on which the supposedly civilized communities of Europe persisted in turning their backs. He visited and re-visited the prisons of Great Britain and many prisons and lazarettos on the continent. His books contain plans of those prisons on which he was able to report favourably, as well as ideal plans of his own. His success after his first publication was immediate, leading to important legislation in England in 1779 and a period of energetic reform which by the year of his death, 1790, had completely changed the situation.

Not all the prisons which Howard inspected before 1777 were beyond redemption. There was, for instance, the purpose-built S. Michele prison in Rome, designed by Carlo Fontana in 1702–03. This was a 'house of correction' for young offenders and consisted of two parallel blocks of cells with a large work-room between where the prisoners' daylight hours were spent. In England there were the 'Bridewells', taking their name, characteristically, from a derelict royal palace in London where the first of them was established. But these 'houses of correction' for lesser offenders tended to fall into the same condition of neglect and indiscipline as the common gaols. In Flanders, there was the 'Maison de Force' near Ghent, begun in 1772 as the central 'house of correction' for the whole country. This was built on a radical plan comparable to some of the hospital plans proposed in France to replace the Hôtel Dieu after the fire of 1772. It was probably the most 'advanced' prison building in Europe before the period of Howard's influence.

London's Newgate, rebuilt in 1770–85 might be cited as another favourable example. It consisted of three courtyards within an extended windowless enclosure and Howard seems to have accepted it

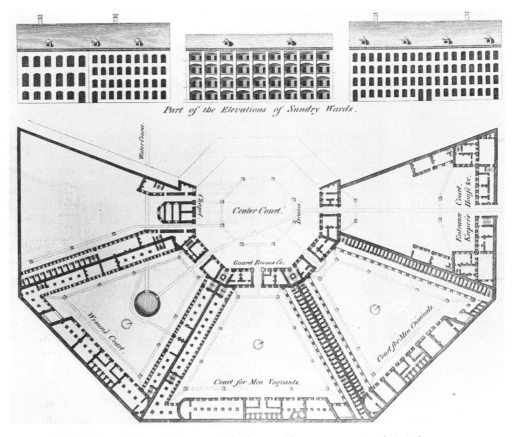

Part of the Elevations of Sundry Wards.

144 The 'Maison de Force' (i.e. prison) built near Ghent, 1772–75, to designs by Malfaison and Kluchman. This plan appealed strongly to the prison reformer John Howard because it aimed at rehabilitation rather than punishment. The illustration is from Howard's *State of the Prisons*, 1777.

as adequate. Newgate however has a claim to distinction in another direction. It seems to have been the first prison in Europe to take the aesthetic factor into account. The S. Michele prison and the Maison de Force at Ghent, although planned by architects, seem to have presented a wholly utilitarian appearance. George Dance the younger, the City of London architect, approached his task differently, attempting to make a grave sort of poetry out of his subject. Inspired, perhaps, by Piranesi's nightmare *Carceri* etchings he used Giulio Romano's style of rustication to produce a mood of solemnity with a

137

 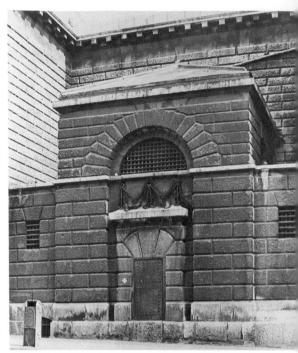

145, 146 Prisons could be powerful examples of *architecture parlante*, that is, the expression through design of the building's function. Piranesi's nightmare *Carceri* (left) find an echo in the dramatic overtones of Dance's Newgate (right) of 1770–85, with its grim rustication and iron shackles above the entrances.

touch of horror; a notably menacing accent being provided by festoons composed of actual iron shackles. Newgate was imitated in a few English provincial gaols but by the end of the century a 'baronial' style (inherited, of course, from the medieval castles commonly used as gaols) had come to be preferred, as, for instance by Robert Adam in his Bridewell on Calton Hill, Edinburgh, 1791–95. Nevertheless the Newgate style found its way to the New World where, in the prison at Richmond, Virginia, Latrobe marked the entrance with iron festoons in 1796. In France, the *architecture parlante* of C.-N. Ledoux was a natural destination for such imaginative excursions, his design for a prison at Aix-en-Provence striking a peculiarly sinister note with corner pavilions treated as gigantic sarcophagi.

Meanwhile the more practical issues raised by Howard's books began to take effect. In England, Parliament passed the Penitentiary Act for the Regulation of Prisons in 1779 and in 1782 a competition was held for plans for male and female prisons. The prize went to a young architect, a silver-medallist of the Royal Academy, William Blackburn. Blackburn was immediately inundated with commissions for gaols, designing no fewer than seventeen before his death at the age of forty in 1790. Some of these involved the *Panopticon* principle, introduced by Jeremy Bentham, and consisting of a circular or semi-

147　Benjamin Latrobe's plan for a prison at Richmond, Virginia, 1796. The cells and workshops surround a semi-circular court. Communal offices such as baths, kitchens and the like are accommodated in the blocks round the subsidiary courtyards flanking the entrance.

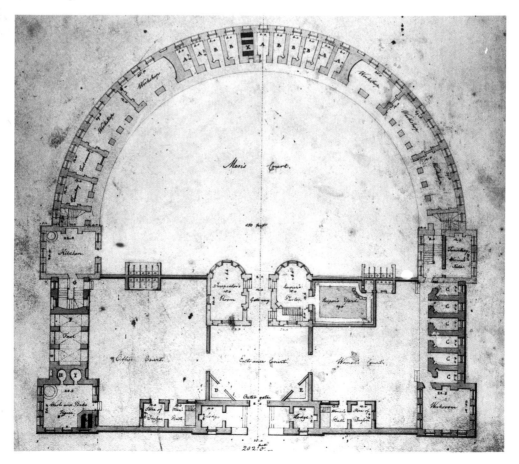

circular structure with cells round the periphery and an observation post at the centre. All Blackburn's designs have a strong feeling for architectural character, partly inherited from Newgate. Of his executed buildings, the gaol at Northleach, Gloucestershire, is partly preserved.

The gaol as a symbol and not merely a device to restrict the freedom of malefactors was characteristic of the late 18th century. In the 19th it soon lost its aesthetic appeal, Holloway gaol, London, 1849–51, being the last to attempt a sinister character, merging the punitive with the Picturesque.

The architecture of commerce

The architecture of commerce is a classification which does not emerge very clearly till near the end of the century, when it is marked by some new and interesting departures. Exchanges and banks are the main subjects of enquiry. Of these, exchanges had the longest architectural ancestry; in 1700 the most famous European exchanges were those of Antwerp, Amsterdam and London, all three built in the

148 Northleach Gaol, Gloucestershire, designed by the great prison architect William Blackburn, 1787–91. Behind the classical façade, the building was laid out in a fan shape with cells round an open courtyard. This was Jeremy Bentham's 'Panopticon' principle.

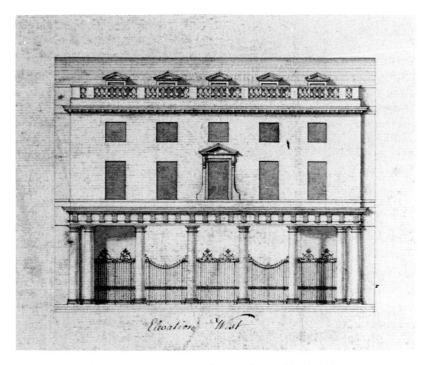

149 London's first corn exchange in Mark Lane, designed by the elder Dance in 1749. Behind the Palladian façade, with its colonnades and wrought iron railings, was a courtyard where the business was conducted.

16th or 17th centuries and still in use in 1800. New exchanges of no distinct architectural significance were built in Rotterdam in 1720, Cologne in 1727 and Bordeaux in 1736.

These exchanges served every kind of marketing transaction, but with the increased diversification of business, groups of merchants found it expedient to hive off into specialized exchanges, e.g. for corn, coal, or later on for stocks and shares. London got its first corn exchange in 1749–50, when the elder Dance designed a building in Mark Lane with a Palladian frontage and, following the tradition of earlier exchanges, a courtyard behind. It was rebuilt in 1827. In Paris a corn exchange on an altogether grander scale was built in 1763–68. This was the innovating building known as the Halle au Blé, a circular structure with concentric external and internal arcades and a circular Doric colonnade running between them. The central space was open until 1783 when Le Grand and Molinos covered it with a timber dome, replaced after a fire in 1808 by Bélanger's iron dome which gave the building its latter-day celebrity. It was demolished in 1885. When a group of Dublin citizens proposed to build an exchange they announced, in 1769, a competition open to the architects of Great Britain and Ireland. It attracted sixty-one entries and was won by Thomas Cooley, a pupil of Robert Mylne, the architect of Blackfriars Bridge. Cooley's design was built (it is now the City Hall). He departed from the tradition of the open court and covered the main space with a coffered dome. The exterior is a refined Palladian composition of decisively 'public' character. The first specialized Stock Exchange was built in London in 1801–2 by the younger Dance's assistant James Peacock. Though a modest enough building,

150 The Halle au Blé (Corn Exchange) in Paris: a pioneering building in several ways. It was built 1763–68 with an open circular courtyard; in 1783 Le Grand and Molinos covered this with a huge timber dome, seen here. In 1813 this was replaced by an even more epoch-making iron and glass dome by Bélanger.

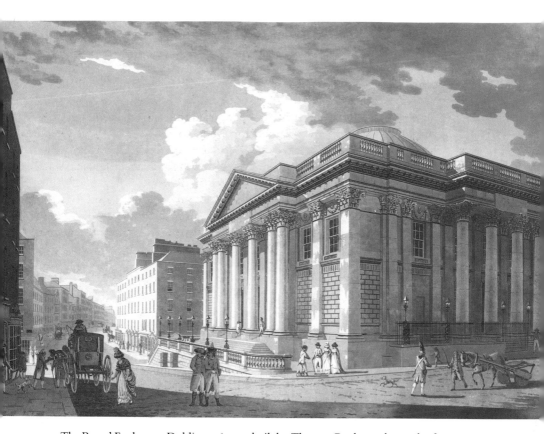

151 The Royal Exchange, Dublin, 1769–79, built by Thomas Cooley as the result of a competition. Pedimented entrance leads into a domed rotunda, just visible in this engraving from James Malton's *Picturesque and Descriptive Views of Dublin*, 1794. It is now the Dublin City Hall, but the original structure survives basically intact.

its plain piers and arches and continuous glazed clerestory suggest the kind of 'reductionism' associated with Dance's Council Chamber in the Guildhall and other of his buildings for the City.

Banks made no appearance on the architectural scene before 1790. From 15th-century Florence onwards banking had been conducted in the residences of bankers and this practice continued into the 19th century. There was, however, one remarkable exception – the Bank of England.

The Bank of England, the prototype of all modern central banks, was founded in 1694. Originally a private bank like any other, its

152 The first Bank of England was built 1732–34 by George Sampson – a series of dignified classical buildings and courts extending back from Threadneedle Street. The main bankers' hall stood between the two courts.

153 The Bank of England Transfer Office, 1765–70, by Sir Robert Taylor. In 1765 the Bank employed Taylor to add new halls and offices, mostly top-lit for security, to Sampson's building.

founder conceived a plan which, within half a century, decisively changed its character. The bank lent the government money to finance its foreign wars and received as interest an annuity payable until the extinction of the debt at an indeterminate date. This was the origin of the 'national debt', which increased with every successive war. The debt was funded and became a mode of investment for a large section of the population. By the end of the Seven Years War in 1763 it had become clear that the national debt was permanent. The management of that debt was in the hands of the Bank of England whose position as banker to the government was consolidated by the end of the century.

This very curt summary is necessary to explain the physical expansion of the Bank's premises. Conducting its business at first in Grocers' Hall, it took over in 1732 the house of its first governor, Sir John Houblon, in Threadneedle Street. Houblon's house was then replaced by a Palladian building on the model of the house attributed to Inigo Jones in Lincoln's Inn Fields. Behind it was a court and behind this a great hall where the Bank's business with the public was conducted: behind this again was another court. As business increased and as the types of 'funds' multiplied the hall became inadequate, so in 1765 the Bank, having acquired more property, employed Robert Taylor to build to the east of the first building. Taylor, who had started his career as a sculptor, was patronised exclusively by City men and had himself served as Sheriff (hence the knighthood). His plan consisted of a domed Rotunda 63 feet in diameter with two rectangular halls to the east, one to the south and another to the north. Each hall took the name of the business transacted in it (Consols Office; 5 per cent Office; Transfer Office; Bank Stock Office). All four were identical in design. There being no precedent for rooms of this kind, Taylor went to James Gibbs's church of St Martin-in-the-Fields and borrowed his system of columns on pedestals supporting timber vaults over nave and aisles. Each hall had sixteen columns. The Rotunda, a clever decorative variation on the Roman Pantheon, seems to have been a 'prestige' piece of no particular use except as an ante-chamber to the four halls. At a later date, Taylor built the magnificent Court Room suite and the Reduced Annuities Office to the west of the original building.

154 Sir John Soane succeeded Taylor as architect to the Bank of England in 1788 and was responsible for a virtual rebuilding that made it one of the great architectural monuments of Europe. This bird's-eye view is not, as is sometimes stated, an exercise in romantic ruination but a careful study in dissection to show the relationship of interior spaces and their construction. Looking from Threadneedle Street, the main

entrance is centre foreground, with the Rotunda further back on the right, and the
Bank Stock Office behind that. Several of Taylor's earlier rooms were allowed to
remain, but Soane encircled the whole site with a single-storey, windowless wall,
which is now nearly all that remains of his work. The view shown here, a tour de force
of architectural draughtsmanship, is the work of J. M. Gandy.

Taylor died in 1788 and was succeeded by the thirty-five-year-old John Soane. By this time Taylor's halls with their obstructive colonnades had evidently been found unsuitable and as they were, in any case, structurally defective, Soane was instructed to rebuild them on the old foundations, and also the Rotunda. The rebuilding was the most creative episode in Soane's career and indeed, one of the most original in European architecture of the time. There is evidence that, at the outset, he had the advice of his former master, George Dance. The Bank Stock Office was the first of the halls to be demolished. In the rebuilding, instead of sixteen points of support it had only four and the form it took approximated to a Byzantine church. This was from one point of view an entirely rational solution but from another a curious divination of treasure-trove in the Dark Ages. The stylistic adventuring may be ascribed to Dance whose 'crude and immature hints' as he called them, which set Soane off on the Byzantine trail, survive in the Soane Museum. Soane proceeded to rebuild the other three halls and the Rotunda in the same style, the last halls being completed in 1818. The halls and Rotunda were demolished in 1925.

155 Soane's Bank Stock Office, 1791–92, a typical exercise in reductionism. This drawing, made under Soane's supervision, shows the room before the clerks' desks were installed. It looks almost like a Byzantine church and there is indeed some evidence of inspiration from the Middle East.

156 Soane's Rotunda of the Bank of England, 1796. Built on the foundation of Taylor's Rotunda, Soane's building dispenses with the normal classical vocabulary and leaves the geometrical forms of the Rotunda to speak for themselves, only slightly accentuated by a pattern of incised lines.

CHAPTER SIX

The Urban Image

Up to now, this essay has concerned itself almost exclusively with individual buildings, whether as examples of architectural style or of building types. Of the composite urban formations which play such an impressive role in the 18th-century panorama nothing has been said. The question now to be asked is whether the division of the century into a Baroque half and a Neo-classical half, proposed as a rough generalization at the beginning of this book, can be effectively retained when we extend our view from individual buildings to groups of buildings and from groups to whole towns. In other words is there 'Baroque town-planning' and 'Neo-classical town-planning'? This is not an easy question. Towns of consequence, whatever the style of their dominating monuments, are in general much older than the 18th century and absolutely new towns are necessarily very rare. What we *can* discern is a change of attitude to the nature of towns – to the urban image. At the beginning of the century a town was regarded as an irreducible fact of nature – something which might be artificially limited or extended and into which new elements might be inserted but not as a totality capable of reorganization and improvement as such. By the middle of the century a more comprehensive attitude has emerged.

The insertion of new, planned, elements into existing cities we can see in both Rome and Paris. In Rome, the Piazza S. Ignazio, formed in 1727 by Filippo Raguzzi, is a tiny enclosure (much smaller than the typical London square) consisting of a few houses laid out round a central block with a concave façade. The elliptical concavity of this central block is echoed in the façades of houses recessed between streets on either side of it so that the whole of the side of the enclosure is on the

157 The Spanish Steps, Rome, with S. Trinità dei Monti at the top. The steps were laid out by Francesco de Santis, 1723–25, as part of a continuing programme of urban embellishment. The insertion of isolated scenographic features in an urban plan is typically Baroque; Neo-classical taste looked more to the grand vista.

move. The other three sides of the piazza are straight but Raguzzi's ornaments confirm the whole as a Rococo enterprise.

On a much grander scale but still Rococo in conception are the Spanish Steps in Rome, leading from the Corso to S. Trinità de' Monti. Designed by Francesco de Santis in 1723–25, this phased ascent of nearly one hundred steps takes the theme of Vignola's stepped approach to the Castello Farnese, expands and elaborates it and transposes its straight lines into a counterpoint of curvatures with wonderful scenic effect.

Planning and politics

In Paris in 1761, Pierre Patte published a plan of the city on which are marked a number of schemes by various architects for monumental *places* in honour of Louis XV. Each scheme is an individual, limited proposal but when distributed on the map they adumbrate something like a monumentalization of the whole city. Even more striking as evidence of the new comprehensive attitude is John Gwynn's plan for the reorganization of London in his *London and Westminster Improved* of 1761. This is, in a sense, Patte in reverse. Patte shows a number of separate monumental conceptions distributed on the existing map. Gwynn takes the existing map and by an elaborate system of street 'improvements' conducts the whole towards a certain degree of monumentality – what he calls 'Public Magnificence'. The differences between Patte and Gwynn demonstrate exactly the passage from one urban image to another – from the Baroque idea of dramatically planned features inserted into a town to the Neo-classical idea of a town considered as an organism capable of connected visual re-creation.

Baroque town-planning is necessarily related to the structures which figure most prominently in the Baroque age – the palace and the great church. But most conspicuously the palace. Among the palaces of the 17th century which served as models for the 18th, the Palace of Versailles takes absolute precedence. At Versailles, the successive labours of Le Vau, Le Nôtre and Jules Hardouin-Mansart had brought into existence not only a palace commanding the almost limitless vistas of a geometrically ordered park but, on the approach side of the palace, a town of corresponding regularity. Park on the

158 Piazza S. Ignazio, Rome, 1727, by Filippo Raguzzi. This is architecture's closest approach to a Baroque stage-set, its concave façades leading the eye to mysterious diagonal views.

west, town on the east, both converged upon the palace. Louis XIV died in 1715. In the same year Karl Wilhelm, Margrave of Baden-Durlach, began to lay out a Versailles of his own at Karlsruhe. It was designed for him by his military engineer, von Betzendorf. Here the wooded park is on the north, the town on the south of the palace. The radial ideal of Versailles is intensely exaggerated, no fewer than thirty-two avenues converging on the central octagonal tower of the palace, and the palace itself shooting its wings into two of the urban radii. There is nothing here of the high sophistication of Versailles and Karlsruhe is a curiosity in which we may perhaps detect a survival of the 'ideal' city plans of the Italian renaissance.

Karlsruhe was never closely imitated, though the converging streets of Neustrelitz, laid out from 1733, and those of another

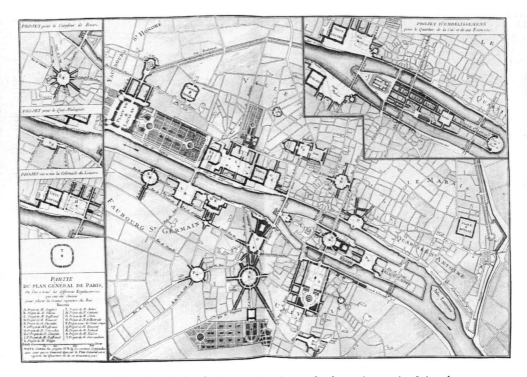

159 Pierre Patte's plan for Paris, 1765, aims at the dramatic surprise. It involves over twenty projects for *places royales* containing statues of Louis XV, each a Baroque explosion which virtually ignores the existing street pattern.

Karlsruhe (Pokoj) in Upper Silesia are in much the same spirit and geometrically dependent on the princely palace. At Ludwigsburg, near Stuttgart, another *residenzstadt*, the new town built by Duke Eberhard Ludwig of Württemberg from 1709, is not subordinated to but laid out alongside the palace. In Spain the Aranjuez lay-out of 1748–78, for Philip V, stems directly from Versailles, with avenues radiating into the park on the west and into a newly planned town on the east. These radiating avenues appear again in St Petersburg, though here – in what used to be called the Nevsky, Admiralty and Ascension Prospects – they converge not on a royal palace but on the Admiralty building.

The emphatic visual dependence of a street plan on a building in which supreme authority is vested is a Baroque idea. Often the

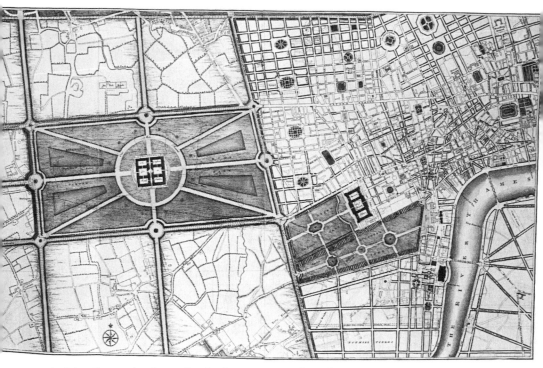

160 John Gwynne's scheme for the improvement of London, 1766, represents a totally different ideal: the modification of an entire city to embody rational and continuous order, with a royal palace exactly in the centre of Hyde Park.

emphasis is of a purely symbolic kind and fades out quickly as we lose sight of the palace. Similar in spirit is another Baroque device – the *place royale*. This developed in France. The *place royale* is not normally dependent on a palace but is simply a formal area in a city, dedicated to the prestige of the monarchy and providing at its centre a site for a statue of the monarch. The first *place royale* was the one built in Paris under Henri IV and called Place Royale until it became Place des Vosges. Under Louis XIV came the circular Place des Victoires and the octagonal Place Vendôme. Under Louis XV came a number of *places royales* in the French provinces – at Rennes, after a great fire in 1720, at Montpellier and at Bordeaux, where the magnificent Place de la Bourse, designed in 1733 by J. J. Gabriel, makes a great spectacle on the bank of the Garonne.

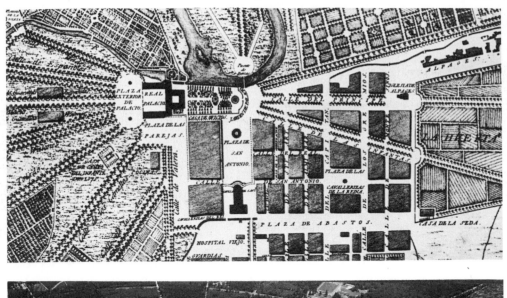

161 Upper left: the park of Aranjuez, south of Madrid, laid out for Philip V of Spain. As at Versailles, the palace is set between park and town, with lines radiating out into both.

162 Lower left: Versailles' radial plan was carried to its ultimate extreme at Karlsruhe, Germany, where no fewer than thirty-two avenues converge upon the royal palace.

163 Above: the Place de la Bourse, Bordeaux, 1733, by J. J. Gabriel, a municipal showpiece facing the river Garonne.

Related in some respects to Bordeaux is the most famous *place royale* of all – the Place de la Concorde in Paris. Today, we are so accustomed to thinking of this space as a component – indeed, the central component – of the great formal framework on which the whole map of Paris hangs that we forget that in origin it was nothing of the kind. It started with a scheme of 1748 promoted by the civic authorities for a 'Place Louis XV' to honour the sovereign (this was the theme of Patte's plan already mentioned). The site was settled by Louis' gift of the ground westward of the Tuileries. A competition was then held (1753) for the lay-out but the final design was in large measure the work of Jacques-Ange Gabriel, son and successor of the Gabriel who designed the *place* at Bordeaux. His two magnificent palaces flanking the Rue Royale with the vista to the Madeleine originally commanded a space with a statue of Louis XV in the centre,

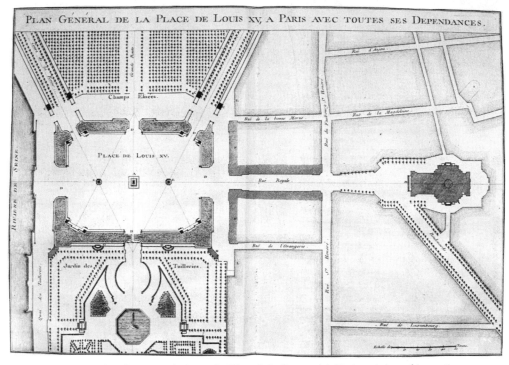

PLAN GÉNÉRAL DE LA PLACE DE LOUIS XV, A PARIS AVEC TOUTES SES DEPENDANCES.

164, 165 The Place Royale (now the Place de la Concorde), Paris, originated in 1748 as a project for honouring Louis XV. It was built from 1753 onwards on the axis of the Tuileries and the Champs Elysées, creating a new axis and new vistas – one between symmetrical buildings by J.-A. Gabriel to the church of the Madeleine, the other to the bank of the Seine where the Pont de la Concorde was later built.

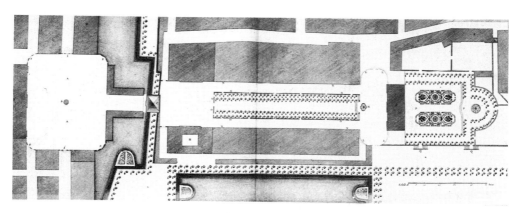

166, 167 The sequence of spaces created at Nancy, in Lorraine, forms one of the most satisfying of all 18th-century exercises in town-planning. From the Place Stanislaus (foreground in photograph, left on the plan), a triumphal arch leads into a long open space, formerly a tilting ground, with the ducal palace at the end. From Héré de Corny, *Plans et elevations de la Place Royale de Nancy*, 1793.

bounded on all four sides by sunk gardens in relation to which the eight seated statues representing French towns were appropriately sited. It was only with the coming of the Pont de la Concorde in 1788–90 and the creation of the Rue de Rivoli under Napoleon that the Place de la Concorde lost its stately gardened isolation and became in due course the whirling centre of a planned Paris.

Contemporary with the Place de la Concorde is the Place Stanislas at Nancy, the capital of Lorraine. Here, Stanislas Leczinski, former King of Poland and by grace of his son-in-law, Louis XV, Duke of Lorraine, proposed the fitting tribute of a *place royale*. In this case, the *place* itself acquires special importance by its siting on the axis of an ancient tilting-ground at one end of which a palace was already proposed. Stanislas' architect, Héré de Corny, completed the palace (on reduced lines), gave it a forecourt with colonnaded hemicycles to left and right, designed uniform elevations for houses along the old tilting-ground (Place de la Carrière) and closed the far end of this with a triumphal arch, through which is entered the Place Royale (Place Stanislas). It is a wonderful sequence – perhaps the finest piece of formal town-planning produced in the 18th century. But the lay-out resulted from unique circumstances. Its character is still that of the traditional and limited *place royale* but its felicitous linkage with other emerging formal elements gives it the air of something more, while its architecture – delicately deriving from Versailles and the Louvre and enhanced by superb ironwork – is, in its own right, a minor masterpiece.

The *place royale* idea was not confined to France. We find it magnificently expressed in the Amalienborg at Copenhagen, begun under Frederick V in 1749. The architect was Nicolas Eigtved, a Dane, but the sources are French. Four palaces, much in the style of J.-H. Mansart, lie across the corners of the *place*. Built as family residences by four leading Danish noblemen, they became the property of the Crown in 1794. In the middle of the square is Sally's equestrian statue of Frederick – one of the few statues designed expressly for a *place royale* to survive the rages of revolution. Of the four roads which lead out of the square one directly faces the Frederiks-Kirke with its portico and commanding dome (compare the Place de la Concorde and the Madeleine); another goes in a direct line to the harbour.

168, 169 Two riverside squares. Above: The Amalienburg, at Copenhagen, planned in 1749 with four identical palaces for Danish noblemen in the four corners. Below: The Praça de Comércio in Lisbon, laid out in conjunction with the grid of streets behind it after the earthquake of 1755.

At Brussels, a *place royale* on the French model was begun by the Habsburg Governor of the Netherlands, Charles de Lorraine, in 1766. It proved to be only the beginning of a much grander project which matured ten years later when the Haute Ville was laid out as a formal residential area round the park of the former Ducal Palace. And in Lisbon we have the Praça do Comércio, created on the bank of the Tagus after the great earthquake of 1755. In both these – as, indeed, at Copenhagen – there is a greater awareness of the relationship of the *place royale* to the town as a whole.

Formality dissolves

The theme of the *place royale* is, of course, something totally distinct from the theme of town *extension*. Most great towns of the 18th century tended to increase by the simple process of the sale of land and the building of streets of houses as a form of commercial enterprise. State control was more rigorous in some cases than in others. In Berlin, from 1721, large areas north and south of Unter den Linden were not only planned but to a great extent built by the State, sites being leased with half-built carcases (*immediatbauten*) already on them. In Paris, on the other hand, great private or corporate landowners like the Comte d'Artois, the banker Laborde and the Grand Priors of the Temple developed their lands for profit without very much regard to amenity; amenity in Paris being associated exclusively (apart from the Royal precincts) with the individual *hôtel*, its court and gardens. In London also it was the development of their properties by great families and institutions which created the extensive westward limb which in the course of the century altered the whole outline and balance of the capital.

London, however, developed in a way of its own. It lacked nearly all the great assets of Paris. Palaces were few and mean and lacked extensive formal lay-outs. Public buildings were not approached by lawns and tree-lined avenues. The great churches – even St Paul's – had not the courtesy of a *parvis*. Fountains there were none. And since fortifications had mostly disappeared with the Middle Ages, there could be no *boulevards* to replace them. London had, however, at the beginning of the century adopted a mode of development not without merit. This consisted in the development of streets round *squares.* The first 'square' in London was the arcaded oblong laid out by Inigo Jones at Covent Garden in 1630 and as this has some relationship to the Place Royale (des Vosges) of Henri IV we may perhaps connect, at that stage, the idea of the London square with that of the *place royale*. But once that is admitted we must add that the ideas parted company at once. The London square became simply an element in the economics of estate development. The square, with its railed private garden, was the magnet with which to draw wealthy buyers. That achieved, the streets adjoining the square had, to the less rich, the prestige of proximity to the rich. Lesser streets followed in their grades. Easy access to a church or chapel-of-ease, as also to a market, was essential and both were often specially built. That was the London formula and it worked for a century and a half.

It worked mainly because the Court in London had never had the powerful attraction of that in Paris. Few of the English nobility aspired to great magnificence in their London houses; they were content with miniature splendour in a house in a row. In this they disappointed even their contemporaries. It was confidently supposed that St James's Square, formed soon after 1660, would consist entirely of a few palaces; and when Cavendish Square was laid out in 1717 the same hope prevailed. In each case one or two immense houses were built but no more. The three or four window frontage was enough — at least for those below the rank of duke.

The whole of that part of London, therefore, built between the reigns of Charles II and Victoria consists of a network of streets in which there is a frequency of squares   the squares mostly taking their names from the families to whom the ground belonged, as Bedford Square (Duke of Bedford), Grosvenor Square, Portman Square, Fitzroy Square (family names); or from names associated with the royal house, as Hanover Square, Brunswick Square, Mecklenburgh Square.

Only rarely did the squares of 18th-century London submit to formal architectural control. Of those that did, Bedford Square is the only intact survivor. Nevertheless the idea of a row of houses treated as one palatial composition was present from early in the century and if it did not find much acceptance in London it did so elsewhere in England with dramatic results — namely in Bath.

170 Hanover Square, London, was built 1718–20, and named after the new reigning dynasty. The scene typifies estate development in 18th-century London. The square, with its large but plain brick houses, its railed enclosure, and a church within easy reach, formed the centrepiece.

The extension of Bath from 1727 onwards was a truly extraordinary episode. It arose on the one hand from a sudden upsurge in the popularity of Bath as a centre of fashionable life when the London season closed and on the other from the practical ambition and naïve vision of a young mason-architect, John Wood. Bath was, in origin, a Roman city and it entered the head of John Wood that the exploitation of its new prosperity in building schemes could be matched with a restoration of its antique splendour in architecture. His earliest proposals included a 'forum', a 'circus' and a 'gymnasium'. These features would necessarily resolve themselves, in practice, into groups of ordinary town houses having, in bulk, the form of their nominal prototypes. No 'gymnasium' was ever attempted but a 'forum' was partly built (North and South Parades) and a 'circus' triumphantly completed (the Circus). A square of the London type (Queen Square) was added, with façades of greater architectural pretension than anything yet seen in the capital. After Wood's death in

171 Bath, the fashionable watering place, expanded rapidly between 1725 and 1770. The town as a whole grew freely but retained formality in its elements – crescents, circuses and squares. In this view the Royal Crescent is in the foreground, the Circus further back to the right.

1754, his son of the same name planned further extensions, incorporating in them an invention of his own – the *crescent* or curved terrace. Today, Queen Square, the Circus and Royal Crescent are the chief architectural features of the Georgian city. Highly original in themselves, they are connected in a loose, informal way which admirably fits the hilly site. The elder Wood, though untravelled, seems to have been familiar with Le Nôtre's use of the *rond-point*; he may have known of Mansart's circular Place des Victoires in Paris. For the younger Wood's Crescent it is hard to think of any prototypes at all: even the rather curious designation 'crescent' seems to come from nowhere.

The achievements of the Woods and their followers at Bath influenced urban extension in Britain for the remainder of the century. Every major English town has its crescents and some have circuses. When James Craig made his plan for the New Town of Edinburgh in 1766 he did, indeed, adhere to conventional London

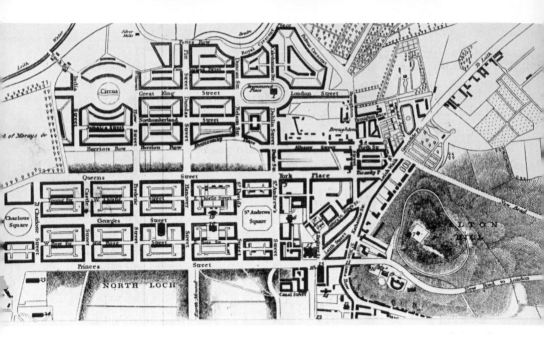

172 Edinburgh New Town was laid out parallel with the old during the latter part of the century. Charlotte Square and St Andrew's Square, each with a prominent building to close the vista, are linked by George Street. North of this is an extension planned after 1800.

practice; but the further development of the New Town after 1800 makes exhaustive use of the Bath elements. John Nash's great plan for Regent's Park and Regent Street of 1811 draws as heavily on the same source. In the United States, there was no planning on the Bath model until 1793, when Charles Bulfinch designed the Tontine Crescent in Franklin Street, Boston, destroyed in 1858. It was a building of Adam-like delicacy, remote from the robust Palladianism of the Bath original.

Growing into the future

It is to America that we must, in conclusion, look to complete this brief survey. In America a wholly new town was necessarily a more realistic proposition than in Europe. William Penn's plan for Philadelphia of 1682 and the plans of Baltimore, Savannah and Reading which followed it in the first half of the 18th century represent the making of new patterns on virgin soil; and the patterns are basically those of a vast military encampment. A slightly greater degree of sophistication comes with the plan of New Orleans made by a French engineer in 1721; an area divided into 66 square plots one of which – the Place d'Armes – provides for the emphatic grouping of church, arsenal and governor's residence, the church being on the axis of a central street. Even more sophistication attaches to Annapolis whose radial plan, adopted shortly before 1700, anticipates Karlsruhe by fifteen years!

But the one great triumph of urban planning in 18th-century America was Washington, D.C. The decision to create a federal capital was taken in 1783. Major Pierre L'Enfant, son of a French painter of battle-pieces, offered his services in a theatrically phrased letter to President Washington in 1789. They were accepted and the site on the Potomac was chosen.

The most striking thing about L'Enfant's plan, seen in historical perspective, is the extent to which it depends on Versailles. Although the basic pattern is a monotonous criss-cross this is overlaid by an arrogant counter-pattern of diagonals. These radiate from the Capitol and again from the White House. More diagonals cross them, meeting them and each other in squares and *ronds-points*, as Le Nôtre's avenues do at Versailles. The Mall before the Capitol echoes the great canal at Versailles and even the relation of Capitol to White House is approximately that of the Palace of Versailles and the Grand Trianon. It is curious, on the face of it, that the greatest symbol of absolutism ever constructed should provide so much and so immediately for the capital city of a nation opposed in every respect to the principles which Versailles embodied. But L'Enfant himself saw no objection. To him, the radiating avenues of Washington represented rays of enlightenment reaching out to all parts of the continent; and, at the same time, welcoming paths for all people, at all times, seeking the protection of the Union.

But the Washington plan remains distinctly a Baroque plan and an anomaly in the Neo-classical climate prevailing in America as well as in Europe at the time it was built. What, in other hands, might Washington have become? Perhaps the only architect of the time really equipped for the creation of a new capital city which should be at one and the same time a great symbol and an organism perfectly

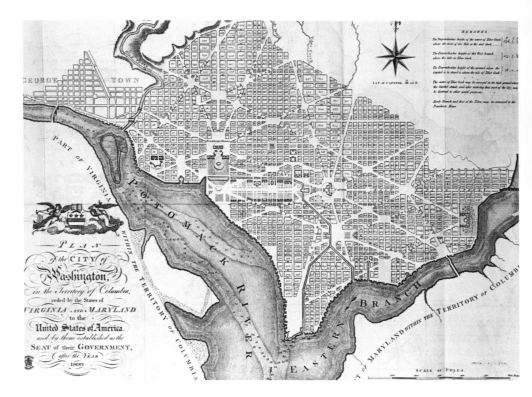

173 When the new republic of the United States decided to create a federal capital in 1783, the plan chosen was curiously close to Versailles, the very symbol of absolutism. It is a combination of grid and radial layout, with the two main vistas, in front of the Capitol and the President's house, meeting on the banks of the Potomac river.

adapted to metropolitan life in a democracy was Claude Nicolas Ledoux. Ledoux never had the opportunity of planning anything on the scale of Washington but he did plan and even partly build, between Arc and Senans, south-west of Besançon, an industrial city of considerable pretension in connection with the state salt-mines. The ruins of its beginnings exist but for the whole conception, richly elaborated in Ledoux's imagination, we must turn to the aerial view in his treatise, already mentioned, of what is there called La Saline de Chaux. Here we see a town laid out, indeed, on a radial principle and with a formal though not over-powering centre. Outside the centre

168

all formality is abandoned. Buildings and groups of buildings lie in the landscape, their forms suited to their varying functions; there is organization but no determination of the plan – it grows into the future as into the distance.

Ledoux's plan for Chaux is one of the great prophetic documents of the 18th century. Its influence was barely felt in his time and it is only in our own day that its combination of the strictly formal with the functionally free has been recognized as a liberating gesture of high import. To compare it with L'Enfant's Washington is perhaps absurd, but in these two plans we have the two great urban images of the end of the century – the one rooted in that heritage of the 17th century which had, all along, so much enriched the 18th; the other a revolutionary flight of the imagination into a new world – a world based on industrial organization and democratic principle, a world from which the potent arrogance of Versailles has at last receded.

174 Ledoux's scheme for the royal salt-works at Chaux – a foretaste of the architect as social engineer. The centre, with the official buildings, conforms to a radial plan, but further out regularity is abandoned and streets are allowed to expand organically. (From Ledoux's *Architecture considerée sous le rapport de l'art* . . ., 1804.)

Select Bibliography

Nations, Regions, Cities, Types

Blunt, A. F.   *Guide to Baroque Rome* (London and Sydney, 1984)

Blunt, A. F.   *Neopolitan Baroque and Rococo Architecture* (London, 1975)

Blunt, A. F.   *Sicilian Baroque* (London, 1968)

Braham, A.   *The Architecture of the French Enlightenment* (London, 1980)

Craig, M.   *Dublin 1660–1860* (Dublin, 1952)

Dainton, C.   *The Story of England's Hospitals* (London, 1961)

Downes, K.   *English Baroque Architecture* (London, 1966)

Fairweather, L.   'The Evolution of the Prison' in *Prison Architecture* (UNSDRI, 1975)

Franz, H. G.   *Bauten und Baumeister der Barockzeit in Böhmen* (Leipzig, 1962)

Gallet, M.   *Paris Domestic Architecture of the 18th Century* (London, 1977)

Hamilton, G. H.   *The Art and Architecture of Russia* (London, 1954)

Hampson, N.   *The Enlightenment* (London, 1968)

Hautecoeur, L.   *Histoire de l'Architecture Classique en France*, vols. iii and iv (Paris, 1951–2)

Hempel, E.   *Baroque Art and Architecture in Central Europe* (Harmondsworth, 1965)

Honour, H.   *Neo-classicism* (Harmondsworth, 1968)

Hussey, C.   *The Picturesque* (London, 1924)

Ison, W.   *The Georgian Buildings of Bath* (London, 1948)

Ives, A. G. L.   *British Hospitals* (London, 1948)

Kalnein, W. and Levey, M.   *Art and Architecture of the Eighteenth Century in France* (Harmondsworth, 1972)

Kauffmann, E.   *Architecture in the Age of Reason* (Harvard, 1955)

Kelemen, P.   *Baroque and Rococo in Latin America* (New York, 2 vols., 1951, 1967)

Kubler, G. and Soria, M.   *Art and Architecture in Spain and Portugal and their American Dominions* (Harmondsworth, 1959)

Kubler, G.   *Portuguese Plain Architecture: between Spices and Diamonds* (Middleton, Conn., USA, 1972)

Lavedan, P.   *Histoire de l'Urbanisme: Renaissance et Temps Moderne* (Paris, 1941)

Leacroft, R.   *The Development of the English Playhouse* (London, 1973)

Lees-Milne, J.   *Baroque in Spain and Portugal and its Antecedents* (London, 1960)

Leistikow, D.   *Ten Centuries of European Hospital Architecture* (Ingelheim, 1967)

Marini, G. L.   *L'Architettura Barocca in Piemonte* (Turin, 1963)

Meekes, C. L. V.   *Italian Architecture 1750–1914* (New Haven, USA, 1966)

Morrison, H.   *Early American Architecture* (Oxford, 1952)

Pevsner, N.   *An Outline of European Architecture* (Harmondsworth, 6th ed. 1965)

Pevsner, N.   *A History of Building Types* (London and Princeton, 1976)

Pinder, W.   *Deutscher Barock, Die Grossen Baumeister des 18 Jahrhunderts* (Leipzig, 1912, 1929)

Pommer, R.   *Eighteenth Century Architecture in Piedmont* (New York and London, 1967)

Rykwert, J.   *The First Moderns: the architects of the Eighteenth Century* (Cambridge Mass. and London, 1980)

Summerson, J.   *Architecture in Britain 1530–1830* (Harmondsworth, 1953; 7th ed. 1983)
Summerson, J.   *Georgian London* (London 1945; 4th ed. 1978)
Thompson, J. D. and Goldin, G.   *The Hospital, a Social and Architectural History* (New York and London, 1975)
Tidworth, S.   *Theatres: an Illustrated History* (London, 1973)
Wittkower, R.   *Art and Architecture in Italy, 1600–1750* (Harmondsworth, 1958; 2nd ed. 1965)
Wittkower, R.   *Studies in Italian Baroque* (London and New York, 1975)
Wethey, H. E.   *Colonial Architecture and Sculpture in Peru* (Harvard, 1949)

Architects

Bolton, A. T.   *The Architecture of R. and J. Adam* (2 vols., London, 1922)
Braunfels, W.   *François de Cuvilliés* (Würzburg, 1938)
Dale, A.   *James Wyatt* (Oxford, 1956)
Downes, K.   *Hawksmoor* (London, 1959)
Du Prey, P. de la R.   *John Soane: the Making of an Architect* (Chicago, 1982)
Fichera, F.   *Luigi Vanvitelli* (Rome, 1937)
Fleming, J.   *Robert Adam and his Circle* (London, 1962)
Franz, H. G.   *Die Kirchenbauten des Dientzenhofer* (Brno, 1941)
Freeden, M. H. von   *Balthasar Neumann* (Munich, 1953)
Friedman, T.   *James Gibbs* (New Haven and London, 1984)
Grimschitz, B.   *Johann Lucas von Hildebrandt* (Vienna and Munich, 1932)
Guinness, D. and Sadler, J. T.   *Mr. Jefferson, Architect* (New York, 1973)
Hamlin, T.   *B. H. Latrobe* (Oxford, 1955)
Harris, J.   *Sir William Chambers* (London, 1970)
Heckmann, H.   *Daniel Pöppelmann; Leben und Werk* (Berlin, 1972)
Herrmann, W.   *Laugier and 18th century French Theory* (London, 1973)
Kimball, F.   *Thomas Jefferson, Architect* (New York, 1968)
Ladendorf, H.   *Andreas Schlüter* (Berlin, 1937)
Marionneau, C.   *Victor Louis, Architecte du Théâtre de Bordeaux* (Bordeaux, 1881)
Monval, J.   *Soufflot* (Paris, 1918)
Otto, C. F.   *Space into Light: the Churches of B. Neumann* (New York, 1979)
Raval, M. and Moreau, J. C.   *Ledoux* (Paris, 1945; 2nd ed. 1956)
Reuther, H.   *Balthasar Neumann, der Mainfrankische Barockbaumeister* (Munich, 1983)
Rosenau, H.   *Boullée and Visionary Architecture* (London and New York, 1976)
Rotili, M.   *Vita di Luigi Vanvitelli* (Naples, 1975)
Sedlmayer, H.   *Johann Bernard Fischer von Erlach* (Vienna and Munich, 1956)
Streichhan, A.   *Knobelsdorff und das Friderizianische Rokoko* (Berlin, 1932)
Stroud, D.   *Capability Brown* (London, 1950)
Stroud, D.   *George Dance* (London, 1971)
Stroud, D.   *Sir John Soane, Architect* (London, 1984)
Stutchbury, H. E.   *The Architecture of Colen Campbell* (Manchester, 1967)
Tadgell, C.   *Ange Jacques Gabriel* (London, 1978)
Voss, K.   *Arkitekten Nikolai Eigtved* (Copenhagen, 1971)
Wilton-Ely, J.   *The Mind and Art of G. B. Piranesi* (London, 1978)
Whistler, L.   *Sir John Vanbrugh, Architect and Dramatist* (London, 1938)

Photographic Acknowledgments

Aerofilms 171; Alinari-Anderson 1; Archives Photographiques, Paris 61, 96; B. T. Batsford Ltd 146; Bildarchiv Foto Marburg 12, 23, 25, 42, 49, 52, 55; Bulloz 6, 60, 97; Yvan Butler, Geneva 68; Copyright Country Life 20, 82, 98; Danish Tourist Board 168; Dresden: Deutsche Fotothek 17, 79, 80; Staatliche Kunstsammlungen 17; German National Tourist Office 133; Giraudon 63, 92, 94, 107, 163; Gloucestershire Record Office 148; Graziano Gasparini 72; Pilot-Photographer R. Henrard 166; Peter Hayden 27, 28; Hirmer Fotoarchiv Munich 33, 46, 54; Martin Hürlimann 29, 110; Karlsruhe: Bildstelle der Stadt 162; A. F. Kersting 5, 21, 58, 67, 73, 74, 77, 78, 88, 91, 100, 129, 131; Emily Lane 41, 59; London: The Governor and Company of the Bank of England 152; British Architectural Library, RIBA 132, 145; British Library 89, 101, 102, 164; British Museum 170; Department of the Environment 90; Guildhall Library 153; By courtesy of Trustees of the Sir John Soane's Museum 125, 149, 154, 155, 156; Thomas Coram Foundation for Children 141; Mansell-Alinari 136, 158; Mansell-Anderson 2, 3, 56; Mansell Collection 106, 157; Mas 65, 66; Maryland Historical Society 113; Georgina Masson 9, 30, 31; Milan: Museo Teatrale alla Scala 119; Tony Morrison South American Pictures 69; Paris: Bibliothèque Nationale 7, 93, 150; Musée Carnavalet 123; Alexandr Paul 39; G. Rampazzi 57; Royal Commission on Historical Monuments (England) 75, 138, 143; Sandak 112, 113; Helga Schmidt-Glassner 15, 48, 70, 71, 114, 115, 116, 118, 120, 121, 122, 126, 128, 130; Toni Schneiders 16, 19, 34, 43, 45, 47, 127; Otto Siegner 169; Edwin Smith 4, 18, 22, 24, 26, 103, 105, 108; Stockholm: Nationalmuseum 117; Rådhus 14; Stadsmuseum 14; Vienna: Kunsthistorisches Museum 10; Roger-Viollet 135; Virginia State Library 147; John Webb 99.

Index

Numbers in italics refer to the illustrations and their captions